Access to History
General Editor: Keith Randell

France 1914-1969: The Three Republics

Peter Neville

Hodder & Stoughton

A MEMBER OF THE HODDER HEADLINE GROUP

The cover illustration is a photograph of Charles de Gaulle (Magnum Photos, London).

To my wife

British Library Cataloguing in Publication Data

Neville, Peter
     France, 1914-69: Three Republics. –
     (Access to History Series)
     I. Title II. Series
     944.081

ISBN 0-340-56561-6

First published 1995

Impression number	10	9	8	7	6	5	4	3	2	1
Year		1999	1998	1997	1996	1995				

Typeset by Sempringham publishing services, Bedford
Printed in Great Britain for Hodder & Stoughton Educational,
a division of Hodder Headline Plc, 338 Euston Road, London NW1 3BH
by Redwood Books, Trowbridge, Wiltshire

Contents

Preface

To the general reader

Although the *Access to History* series has been designed with the needs of students studying the subject at higher examination levels very much in mind, it also has a great deal to offer the general reader. The main body of the text (i.e. ignoring the Study Guides at the ends of chapters) forms a readable and yet stimulating survey of a coherent topic as studied by historians. However, each author's aim has not merely been to provide a clear explanation of what happened in the past (to interest and inform): it has also been assumed that most readers wish to be stimulated into thinking further about the topic and to form opinions of their own about the significance of the events that are described and discussed (to be challenged). Thus, although no prior knowledge of the topic is expected on the reader's part, she or he is treated as an intelligent and thinking person throughout. The author tends to share ideas and possibilities with the reader, rather than passing on numbers of so-called 'historical truths'.

To the student reader

There are many ways in which the series can be used by students studying History at a higher level. It will, therefore, be worthwhile thinking about your own study strategy before you start your work on this book. Obviously, your strategy will vary depending on the aim you have in mind, and the time for study that is available to you.

If, for example, you want to acquire a general overview of the topic in the shortest possible time, the following approach will probably be the most effective:

1 Read chapter 1 and think about its contents.
2 Read the 'Making notes' section at the end of chapter 2 and decide whether it is necessary for you to read this chapter.
3 If it is, read the chapter, stopping at each heading to note down the main points that have been made.
4 Repeat stage 2 (and stage 3 where appropriate) for all the other chapters.

If, however, your aim is to gain a thorough grasp of the topic, taking however much time is necessary to do so, you may benefit from carrying out the same procedure with each chapter, as follows:

1 Read the chapter as fast as you can, and preferably at one sitting.
2 Study the flow diagram at the end of the chapter, ensuring that you understand the general 'shape' of what you have just read.

3 Read the 'Making notes' section (and the 'Answering essay questions' section, if there is one) and decide what further work you need to do on the chapter. In particularly important sections of the book, this will involve reading the chapter a second time and stopping at each heading to think about (and to write a summary of) what you have just read.
4 Attempt the 'Source-based questions' section. It will sometimes be sufficient to think through your answers, but additional understanding will often be gained by forcing yourself to write them down.

When you have finished the main chapters of the book, study the 'Further Reading' section and decide what additional reading (if any) you will do on the topic.

This book has been designed to help make your studies both enjoyable and successful. If you can think of ways in which this could have been done more effectively, please write to tell me. In the meantime, I hope that you will gain greatly from your study of History.

Keith Randell

Acknowledgements

The Publishers would like to thank the following for permission to reproduce illustrations in this volume:

Cover - Charles de Gaulle, Magnum Photos, London
Collection Viollet, Paris p. 46; Imperial War Museum, London p. 83; Lapi-Viollet, Paris p. 88; Hulton Deutsch Collection, London p. 127.

Every effort has been made to trace and acknowledge ownership of copyright. The Publishers will be glad to make suitable arrangements with any copyright holders whom it has not been possible to contact.

CHAPTER 1

Introduction

A stereotyped view of France in the years before 1914 might conjure up images of the Can-Can, the Folies Bergéres musical hall, the Impressionist school of painters (including great figures such as Manet and Toulouse Lautrec), and a whiff of decadence. An association with decadence was also to pervade much of the period between 1914 and 1969.

This was not just a matter of sexuality, whereby provincial, conservative France was wrongly associated with permissive, colourful Paris, but of governmental scandal and incompetence as well. In the 1880s and 1890s there were the Panama Scandal (about fraudulent dealings associated with the building of the Panama Canal) and the Dreyfus Affair (when a Jewish army officer was unfairly accused of treason). Similarly, the 1930s had the Stavisky Affair (see page 43) which centred around the suicide of a well-known gangster, and scandal continued to be a feature of French political life.

Another common theme which ran through French politics was apparent political instability. Governments came and went, at least up until the establishment of the Fifth Republic in 1958, with bewildering rapidity. This has variously been ascribed to unworkable constitutions, corruption, the quarrelsome nature of French politicians, class antagonism, and a legacy of revolutions stretching back to 1789 (there were also revolutions in France in 1830, 1848 and 1871).

The fluctuation of economic cycles will also be a theme of this study, which will highlight the differences in economic performance between the Third Republic and its successors. There were constant devaluations of the franc and the currency was only really stabilised after 1958.

Attention will also be paid to the twin themes of defeat and occupation. In 1870-1 France had been defeated and occupied by the Germans, and although she avoided defeat in the war of 1914-18, her northern provinces were devastated by German occupation. In 1940 she was catastrophically defeated by Nazi Germany, occupied, and also ruled (in part) by a quasi-fascist regime which brought shame to the name of France. Even after the end of the Second World War, France was to suffer defeat and humiliation in colonial wars in Indo-China and Algeria. Yet through all these humiliations and setbacks the French people retained their sense of separateness and national identity.

Another feature of the period was the French tendency to revert to authoritarianism in crisis, and to rally around the person of an aged warrior or politician. In 1917 at a moment of crisis in the First World War France found such a man in Georges Clemenceau, in 1940 the saviour (less creditably) was seen to be Pétain, and in 1958 Charles de Gaulle. But paradoxically France has remained a democracy, even if at times the foundations of that democracy have seemed flimsy.

1 France and the Historians

Historians have found fascinating themes in twentieth-century French history. The most important of these have been: the bloodshed and sacrifice of the First World War, the apparent mismanagement and defeatism of the inter-war period, the catastrophic 'fall of France' in 1940, the loss of an empire in the years after 1945, and the dominant role of Charles de Gaulle in the first years of the Fifth Republic after 1958.

Some writers, such as J.P. Duroselle and René Girault, have seen the disaster of 1940 as the result of a long period of French political and economic decline, leading by the late-1930s to decadence in France's political life and institutions. Others, such as Robert Young who believes that France showed distinct signs of recovery in 1938-9, have disagreed with this interpretation. The historical debate about this controversial issue will be followed through in the pages of this book.

In the post-war period the case for rule by a dominant authoritarian figure such as Charles de Gaulle has been put by historians like Laucouture and Jackson. They have done this while attempting to place Gaullism in the broader stream of France's democratic tradition.

For historians France has often been a paradox in the twentieth century. Contrasts have been drawn between it being heroic in the defence of its democracy at one moment (as in 1914-18) and apparently despairing in its acceptance of Nazi domination at another (in 1940); and economically feeble and archaic for long years between 1918 and 1939, yet vibrant and technologically impressive for decades after 1945. In the pages that follow the factors behind these apparent paradoxes should become clearer.

2 France in 1914

In July 1914 France was on the eve of a life and death struggle with the German empire - a struggle both to win back the provinces of Alsace and Lorraine which had been lost to Germany in 1871, and to preserve the balance of power in Europe. What was the France of 1914 like?

Again elements of paradox and ambiguity are evident. In terms of artistic, and some areas of economic achievement, France was vibrant, and she also had the second largest colonial empire in the world, but in a most basic area, her weakness was highlighted by German strength. France in 1914 had a population of only 39.6 millions against Germany's 64.9 millions. This represented a population growth of only 9.7 per cent since 1871 whereas Germany's population had increased by over 57 per cent. In industrial performance, too, France lagged behind the other industrial powers. In 1913, for example, French industrial production accounted for only 6.4 per cent of total world production against figures of twice that size for Great Britain and Germany. Although in 1900 her merchant marine was the fourth largest in the world, half of this fleet was under sail in an age of steampower. Yet historians have commented on the pride French people had in their solid peasantry, their large gold reserves, their diplomatic and military influence (until 1856 all European treaties had been drawn up in French, and it was still the language of European diplomacy), their artistic achievement, and their colonial empire.

a) The Class System

This pride reflected a dogged conservatism and an innovatory brilliance, both of which could be seen at work in the French class system before 1914.

i) The Peasantry

In 1914 most French men and women were still peasants. Many people thought of the peasantry as the glory of the nation, for they represented in their lifestyles the virtues of thrift, hard work, patriotism and (often) simple religious piety in following their Catholic faith. Large farms were unusual in France before 1914, and subsistence farming on small acreage in provinces like Provence, Brittany and Champagne was the norm. Elsewhere in western and central France, agricultural work was carried out by *métayers* (share croppers) who provided the labour for landowners and sometimes capital and equipment as well, although the *métayers* were usually too poor to provide both cash and equipment. In 1913 the average size of a *métairie* (the farm on which the sharecropper worked) was 50 to 60 hectares but there was immense variety. In some rural areas the *métairie* could be as small as 2 hectares, in other areas the average size could be as much as 100 hectares. But whatever the size of the farm-holding, the system of sharecropping was innately conservative and authoritarian. A handbook on sharecropping in 1882 said 'The first duty of a *métayer* is to obey.' Obedience meant accepting the authority of the landowning class over the peasantry. While it has been pointed out that sharecropping gave a hard-working peasant a chance to have his own farm, he usually lacked the money to use the latest techniques, and the landowner (who got only half the profits from it) was invariably too mean to improve it. The sharecropper was rarely allowed much dignity. In one recorded instance, the landowner merely referred to his sharecropper as *'Chose'* (thing) because he could never remember his name! The same landlord allegedly said, 'Never bother me with requests for repairs: I do none on principle.' The *métayer* often felt like a slave.

Wine growers were more independent spirits. They had a long

tradition of conflict with state and town authorities because of the heavy taxation imposed on their produce. But the rural tradition in France was generally conservative, and the fact that politicians needed the rural vote (most French people still lived in the countryside) made them pander to this conservatism. Thus in the 1890s tariffs were introduced to make foreign foodstuffs more expensive, even though in the long run this discouraged French peasant farmers from introducing new techniques, and encouraged small uneconomic agricultural units which made French agriculture uncompetitive. As it was, despite a slight rise in prices before 1914, French agriculture was in a depressed state in the opening decade of the twentieth century. This was despite a sixfold increase in the use of fertilisers between 1871 and 1914.

ii) Artisans and Workers

This patchy picture repeated itself where industrial workers were concerned. France had been slow to industrialise in the nineteenth century. One result of this was the survival of a class of artisans, highly skilled craftsmen such as printers and jewellery makers, into the early twentieth century. These artisans thought themselves superior to factory workers, and when increasing mechanisation came about in the 1890s they found themselves in increasing conflict with employers.

It is a paradox that, although the artisans looked down on the factory workers, they also tried to get their assistance by organising them into trade unions. Sometimes there was co-operation between the two groups but the factory workers also showed themselves capable of independent action (notably in a series of strikes at the world-famous Le Creusot steelworks).

Life for the factory worker, as for the peasant, was tough. Long hours were worked - 10 to 14 hours a day was the norm - although by 1914 trade unions were demanding an 8-hour working day, and a shorter working week with better working conditions. Historians talk about the 'social question' in France before 1914, and it is true that in the area of social reform, France lagged behind other European states (although there were some concessions like an eight-hour day for the miners in 1905, and old age pensions in 1910). Arguably political issues were more important in France than elsewhere, and this may have diverted attention away from the need for improved welfare for the workers.

Traditionalism in the way workers were treated was paralleled by traditional attitudes in the structure of French industry. Most of the workforce was still engaged in traditional trades such as textiles, clothing and leather, in which the goods produced were often hand made. Even the growing motor industry (led by pioneers like Louis Renault and André Citroën) was at first regarded as a luxury industry before 'Taylorism' (that is mass production techniques) began to spread to France from the USA. However, well into the inter-war period, as later chapters will show, French industry was often small scale and labour intensive.

Another feature of French industry in the period after 1918 was already in evidence before 1914. Old fashioned, labour-intensive industries existed side by side with modern dynamic ones, of which the fastest developers were chemicals, electricity and motor manufacture. This duality in industrial achievement continued to be a feature thereafter, with French technical ingenuity not always being matched by good organisation. Note should also be taken of the steady growth in the French service sector before 1914, which meant, for example, that the big department store began to supersede the small corner shop.

But as far as the French worker was concerned, growing mechanisation seemed to bring with it a dull, brutalised lifestyle with ferocious factory discipline. As the government too began brutally to repress organised labour (troops were not infrequently used against strikers) more and more French workers joined unions and their umbrella organisation, the Confederation Général du Travail (CGT or General Labour Confederation).

iii) The Bourgeoisie

The historian J.F. MacMillan has remarked that the crucial class in French society before 1914 was the lower middle class. There was a clear distinction in France between the lower middle class and the haute bourgeoisie (the upper middle class). In his view the estimated four million small businessmen in France in 1900, most of whom ran family businesses which employed no other workers at all, represented the solid conservative core of the Third Republic at that time (the Third Republic governed France between 1871 and 1940). These petit bourgeois (lower middle class) also included professional groupings such as primary school teachers and low-grade civil servants. People who, by and large, were poorly paid but were acutely aware of their status which placed them above the peasants, artisans and industrial workers. It was often claimed in the period up to 1940 that the Third Republic was the Republic of the 'small men' in the sense that it represented the lower middle class better than any other class in France. Or to put it another way, it allegedly represented the big men in small local fishponds (in a small village the schoolmaster had considerable status).

Other historians have argued that the upper middle class was the dominant class in France before 1914 - and indeed long afterwards as well. This was the class of big bankers, financiers and industrialists which seemed to hold the country's purse strings. The Left in France (initially the Socialists but later the Communists as well) was convinced that the so-called 'two hundred families', the richest members of the upper middle class, held the reins of power. This theory first appeared midway through the nineteenth century in France, but even in the 1930s the socialist prime minister Léon Blum (see page 47) was convinced that this privileged group had cost him his power.

Writing after the Second World War, Blum (using the term 'bourgeoisie' rather loosely, as one historian has pointed out) said: 'Despite all appearances to the contrary, it is the bourgeoisie which has ruled France for the past century and a half.' MacMillan and other modern historians have refuted this 'conspiracy theory', pointing out that relatively few great industrialists or financiers went into politics, and that wealth in France was much more evenly spread outside the so-called 'two hundred families'. There was, for example, a whole class of hundreds of thousands of so-called rentiers, that is people who lived entirely on the interest from their investments in property and stocks and shares. The tendency, too, of interest groups to herd together, like the Comité des Forges (founded 1864) or Committee of Ironmasters, gave them great economic power.

The traditional professions like medicine and the law also wielded considerable political power, with many representatives in Parliament, and this power was self-perpetuating. Only the members of the haute bourgeoisie could afford to give their sons the sort of expensive education needed to become a politician or a top civil servant (the education of girls attracted little attention before 1914). Education was therefore a means of preserving existing class divisions in France.

iv) The Aristocracy

When France ceased to have a monarchy in 1848 the old aristocracy lost all real political power in France. But the aristocracy continued to exist, and to preserve to a large degree its privileged lifestyle. Some made marriage alliances with the grands bourgeois and moved into the world of high finance and business in Paris, while members of the rural aristocracy remained some of the greatest landowners in the country. This was an indication of the essentially conservative, static nature of French society. The old counts, marquises and dukes had lost their political power but they retained their social exclusiveness. The prefix 'de', as in 'de Richelieu', denoted membership of the aristocracy, and some members of the upper middle class were prepared to buy such a title. Even in the middle of the twentieth century there were some 30,000 individuals in France who were genuinely aristocratic, but more tellingly perhaps another 15,000 who falsely claimed to be aristocrats.

b) Politics

Between 1871 and 1940 France was under the form of government known as the Third Republic. Under this system most power lay with the lower house of Parliament (Chamber of Deputies), although the Senate or upper house (elected by indirect suffrage and not based on one man one vote) could sometimes block legislation. The executive power or Presidency was deliberately kept weak, but the presidential role did still depend to a degree on the personality of the office holder. The President did, for example, retain the right to appoint the Prime Minister and sign treaties with foreign states. Study of the period before and after 1914 suggests that nonentities were deliberately elected President by the Chamber. It was the Chamber rather than the French people which had the power to elect the President.

Nevertheless modern historians have stressed that a presumption of constitutional weakness during the period of the Third Republic would be misleading. True, governments did come and go with great rapidity but closer analysis shows that, although the governments changed frequently, their personnel did not. The same small band of politicians were constantly reappointed to office. They merely changed jobs. This was true not only of the Third Republic, but of the Fourth Republic (1946-58) as well.

The most important one is in the political arena, a sphere in which France in the period between 1914 and 1958 at least, appeared to be in a state of constant flux. Here statistics can be deceptive. During the history of the Third Republic, a French prime minister could, on average, expect to hold office for only eight months. Between 1870 and 1940 France had no less than 108 governments, and matters did not greatly improve under the Fourth Republic (the Mendès-France government of 1954-5 holding the record for longevity). Yet Andrew points out that during the 70-year period between 1870 and 1940, 43 per cent of outgoing French government ministers reappeared in the next administration. Of all the Members of Parliament elected under the Third Republic only 10 per cent were really involved in government because the others were never elected for more than two parliamentary terms, that is eight years. This was, Andrew argues, too short a time to make an impact on national politics and get a job in government. The history of French politics under the Third Republic (and the same argument can be applied to the Fourth) can be seen as a case of the same old faces in the same old jobs. Examples of this sort of personal continuity in French politics are given in Chapter 3. This creates what we might call the 'Andrew thesis' that French politics between 1914 and 1940, and again between 1946 and 1958 was about 'stable instability'.

The dominant political party in France before 1914 was the Radical Republicans, although the Socialists were beginning to become important as well. The Right, consisting of Monarchists and Bonapartists (supporters of the family of the former Emperor Napoleon III), was largely discredited by 1900, because of its associations with anti-republican movements and scandals like the Dreyfus Affair. This gave the Radicals a virtual monopoly of power which they used to break the position of Catholicism as the official religion of France in 1905. The Church's hostility to the Republic since its birth in 1871 made this a necessity for the Radical party.

The Radicals identified themselves as the party of the 'small man', petit bourgeois shopkeepers and businessmen, who were noted for their financial prudence and anti-clericalism. But this claim was deceptive as the leadership of the Radical Republicans contained some of the richest men in France, and the party was more notable for its unwillingness to reform the social structure and desire to protect property and privilege. In this sense, the title 'radical' was quite misleading for only in their ferocious dislike of the Catholic Church could the Radicals be said to have merited this description.

Many of the characteristics of the Third Republic are to be found in the Fourth. Despite the efforts of Charles de Gaulle in the early post-war period, France was still saddled with a weak presidency and frequent changes of government. But the historian Christopher Andrew has pointed out that this characteristic can be as misleading for the study of the Fourth Republic as it is for the Third, for although governments came and went at great speed, the ministerial positions were still held by the same men. Governmental instability therefore went hand in hand with ministerial stability (ministers just wore different hats as finance minister, war minister and so on).

In other respects though the history of the Fourth Republic was quite different from that of the Third. The economy boomed in the 1950s in a way quite unlike the inter-war experience. And France's major external problems were colonial, to do with Indo-China and Algeria, rather than mainstream foreign policy ones (such as the threat from Nazi Germany in the 1930s).

It could be argued that throughout the period 1914 to 1969, France was engaged in a search for governmental stability. If this was the case, it is generally true that this was achieved only after the establishment of the Fifth Republic in 1958-9. General de Gaulle altered the constitution to give more power to the President of the Republic, and under his presidency there was greater governmental stability, even if the Prime Minister had less power than under the Third and Fourth Republics.

There is little doubt that the constant changes of government between 1914 and 1958 did hurt the French economy because it created a perception of weakness abroad, so that foreign investors thought twice about placing funds in France, and the franc was all too often a weak currency which was under pressure in the world's financial markets. But the degree of economic prosperity under the Fifth Republic, while real enough, flowed out of the achievement of the Fourth Republic, and this has sometimes been forgotten. What was distinctive about the Fifth Republic was its assertive, nationalistic foreign policy which was closely associated with the personality and beliefs of General Charles de Gaulle.

But historians agree that de Gaulle consciously gave France a colourful and dramatic foreign policy because he wanted to strengthen the stability of his own regime. If, he reasoned, French men and women saw France playing an heroic role abroad, they would be more satisfied with their lot at home. De Gaulle understood the French. Stability was not a natural state in French politics, as the General himself was to learn again in 1968.

Making notes on 'Introduction'

Your aim following a reading of this chapter should be to make certain i) that you have understood the main features of French history in this period, ii) that you are aware of the major issues and arguments concerning it and iii) that you have an understanding of the basic structure of French society in the pre-1914 period.

Now try to write short answers to the following questions, which will show whether you have understood the important points or not.

1   What major themes can you identify in French history between 1914 and 1969?
2   Which classes would you say were dominant in French society before 1914?

This book covers one of the widest historical spans in the whole *Access to History* Series. It is important, therefore, that you are able to identify the major issues in French history in the period between 1914 and 1969. This should not be too difficult if you read the introductory section to this chapter carefully, that is up to Section a) and also Section b).

You will then need to understand as much as possible about each issue. This will involve understanding why historians consider an issue to be important, and how the views of individual historians about the issue differ. Your third task will be to decide which of these views seem to you to be the most plausible. This can sometimes be very difficult, as all the views can appear eminently plausible and it may be difficult to make up your mind which view to support. If you do not find any of the evidence conclusive then it is perfectly in order for you to say so. Historical issues are rarely (if ever) 'black and white', and modern French history has as many controversies and uncertainties in it as any other historical period. Don't be unduly worried if you can't make a definite judgement on an historical problem (e.g. Was France's victory in the First World War really a victory or a defeat? It is a question for serious discussion.)

CHAPTER 2

War and Peace 1914-18

1 The Coming of War

In the years before the outbreak of the First World War in August 1914, Republican France was part of an alliance bloc known as the Triple Entente (France, Britain, Russia) which had been formed between 1894 and 1907. The Entente powers were opposed by Austria-Hungary and Germany which came to be known during the war as the Central Powers (after their central position in Europe). Italy, which was to fight on the side of the Entente powers in the First World War, was actually an ally of the Central Powers before 1914 but changed sides in the hope of gaining territory from Austria-Hungary, and entered the war in 1915. Turkey entered the war on the side of Austria-Hungary and Germany in 1914.

The Entente was a loose agreement about spheres of colonial influence (in 1904 France recognised Britain's dominant position in Egypt, while the British recognised hers in Morocco), but France did have a more binding commitment to Tsarist Russia which went back to 1894. Both countries were committed to aid the other if it were attacked by Germany or her allies. In the so-called 'July crisis' of 1914, the distinction between the Franco-Russian Treaty and the Anglo-French Entente (which did not commit Britain to come to France's aid if she were attacked) was to be very important.

Military planning was a contributory factor to the coming of war in 1914. The French plan was simplicity itself. The so-called Plan 17 provided for a massive attack across the Franco-German frontier to regain the provinces of Alsace-Lorraine. This was precisely what the Germans expected the French to do.

Germany's problem was that she might have to fight a war on two fronts, against France and Russia. When the plan was conceived in the 1890s, it provided for an offensive against Russia in the east and a defensive campaign against France in the west. This emphasis was changed in 1905 so that it was France that was to be attacked first of all, and knocked out of the war in six weeks. The calculation was that the slow-moving Russian army would take so long to mobilise that France would be defeated before it could intervene. So finely tuned was the German Schlieffen Plan (named after its originator Count von Schlieffen) with the departure of troop trains worked out to the very minute, that if a crisis arose between the rival alliance blocs, Germany was virtually committed to attack France without having time to see whether she should honour her alliance with Russia.

What was the likely French reaction? True, France wished to win back the last provinces of Alsace-Lorraine which had been lost in 1870-1 but the French government followed a fairly cautious foreign policy before 1914 and did not show any overwhelming desire for *revanche* (revenge). In 1908, for example, when Austria-Hungary and Russia confronted one another over the issues of who was to rule over the former Turkish provinces of Bosnia-Hercegovina and have control over the Straits between the Black and Mediterranean Seas, France had refused to support her Russian ally. By contrast, Germany had pledged her full support for Austria-Hungary. So French support for Russia in the event of another Balkans crisis was by no means automatic.

Thus, when a Bosnian Serb assassinated the heir to the Austro-Hungarian throne in June 1914, it was still possible that the war which followed might be localised. Austria wanted to punish the Serbs, and Russia would not stand by and see her small, sister Slav state destroyed. What made a wider European war inevitable was the German decision to fight on the side of Austria-Hungary (not actually required under the terms of their 1879 alliance, as Austria-Hungary was the aggressor not the victim), and the Schlieffen Plan which committed the Germans to an all out offensive against the French. When France surprised Germany by withdrawing her forces ten kilometres from their common frontier it made no difference. The die was cast. The German generals had to remind their Emperor William II that they could not, as he naively supposed, merely turn the armies around and march against Russia. German military planning demanded an attack in the west against France, regardless of France's reaction to a war breaking out between Germany and Russia.

The Schlieffen Plan was also of crucial importance in another sense. The Germans had decided that to avoid the fortifications along the Franco-German frontier, they must move a large part of their million-strong army across the flat plains of neutral Belgium. In 1914, the Germans impertinently demanded free passage for their army through neutral Belgium which was refused, but in doing so they broke the 1839 treaty which guaranteed Belgian neutrality. Prussia (as it then was in the days before German unification), France and Britain had all signed the treaty and infringement of it might bring Britain, too, into the European war. The British asked France if she would honour Belgian neutrality in 1914, and the answer was yes. Germany could make no such promise and her invasion of Belgium knowingly took the risk of bringing Britain into the war.

If the French knew precisely what they would do in the event of a war with Germany, they were still, as indicated above, uncertain about what Britain would do. All France had in the way of a commitment from the British was a promise that if war broke out, the Royal Navy would guard the Channel and the North Sea if the French would look after the Mediterranean. There was no assurance that British troops would be sent to France if Germany attacked, but the French tended to assume that such help would be forthcoming. It was a rather dangerous assumption, but in the event the German invasion of Belgium in 1914 gave the British government a pretext for declaring war on Germany on

4 August. By contrast, the Germans had to make up an excuse for attacking France: it was the feeble fabrication that France's air force had bombed Germany. But as we have seen, the demands of the Schlieffen Plan left the German generals little choice.

Could France have stood by and allowed her Russian ally to be defeated by the Austro-German alliance? Many historians have felt that she could not. As it was, German military planning, not France's, forced her into a general European war willy-nilly just as ultimately it brought Britain in, too. The likelihood is that had the Schlieffen Plan taken another form which did not violate Belgian neutrality, France would have been forced to fight to preserve the balance of power in Europe anyway. But the evidence does not suggest that she was in any sense itching for a chance to reverse the verdict of the war of 1870-1.

2 The Sacred Union

In August 1914 France entered the war led by a government of 'sacred union' *(union sacrée)*. This included figures from across the party spectrum: President Poincaré, Briand and Delcassé (the former Foreign Minister) but, importantly, also some Socialists, albeit in junior positions. Given the extent of pre-war political feuding, and the wave of bitterly contested strikes inspired by the Left in 1912-13, this display of political unity was remarkable indeed.

The formation of this government of national unity undoubtedly owed something to the assassination (shortly before the outbreak of war) of the Socialist leader Jean Jaurès who had passionately opposed the introduction of the 1913 army bill which provided for three years' military service for every French man. This made it possible for the Socialists to commit themselves to the war effort. In return, the Minister of the Interior in the 'sacred union' cabinet showed some tact in not arresting a number of left-wing figures who would have been suspect because of their previous pacifism and anti-militarism. Ancient feuds between left- and right-wing politicians ceased in the national interest in August 1914 because *la patrie* (the nation) was in danger.

It is important to note, however, that the success of the idea of 'sacred union' owed much to the widespread assumption in France that the war would soon be over. The French may not have had a memorable phrase like the British one that the war 'would be over by Christmas' but the expectation of a quick victory meant that old arguments about religion (the role of the Catholic Church in French society), the rights of employers and workers, and the role of the army, could temporarily be buried. The 'sacred union' was, in the words of one historian, a political truce. It did not mean that old differences had gone altogether, and once it became clear that victory was not going to be achieved within six months or a year, they were resurrected. This is not surprising. As it was, the existence of the 'sacred union' government contributed to the high morale of France's fighting men as they faced the decisive campaign of 1914.

3 The 1914 Campaign

In August and September 1914 France was to fight a desperate battle for survival, as the German army swept through Belgium and into France's northern departments. At one point, the invaders were 25 kilometres from Paris across the River Marne, and on the verge of victory. There on the Marne, the Germans were repulsed, and though there was a brief moment when a rapid Allied follow-up might have brought a complete breakthrough, both sides dug lines of trenches. This gave the war on the western front its distinctive characteristic of trench warfare. By the end of 1914 there was stalemate in the west.

Two questions therefore need to be asked. Why was France brought to the edge of defeat in 1914, and how did she survive? Part of the answer to the first question lies with the strange strategic delusion that possessed the French High Command in 1911. This was that France, even with inferior population and resources (40 millions to 65 million Germans), could rely on *cran* (guts) and *élan* (spirit) to sweep aside the Germans and drive into Alsace and Lorraine. France's Plan 17 made exactly this assumption.

Much of the blame for this dogmatic belief in the power of attack has been placed on General Foch, and he certainly made statements which give some credence to the accusation. One of the better-known ones was, 'A battle won is a battle in which one will not confess oneself beaten'. But in the 1960s the American historian Barbara Tuchmann pointed out that Foch was not just the simplistic apostle of attacking strategy often portrayed. Indeed he is on record as saying that the idea that fighting spirit alone could win wars was 'an infantile notion'. Whatever Foch's responsibility, it seems clear that the entire French High Command, including the Commander-in-Chief Joffre, was obsessed by 1914 with the idea of all-out attack in Alsace and Lorraine which would bring a speedy victory. To be fair to Joffre, he also considered an offensive through Belgium against Germany, but this was ruled out because it would breach Belgian neutrality.

Such thinking played into the hands of the Germans who were prepared to remain on the defensive in Alsace-Lorraine, while the right wing of their army moved through Luxemburg and Belgium into northern France. The analogy of a swing door can be used here for as the French pushed forward into Alsace-Lorraine, the Germans would swing around behind them to the west of Paris. If the Schlieffen Plan worked, then the French and their British allies would be surrounded in a classic military manoeuvre.

And it nearly did work. First the Germans poured into Belgium, capturing strong points like Liége and the Belgian capital, Brussels.

Then they pressed on into France itself while the French government panicked and made plans to move itself to Bordeaux. At this point the French army needed a miracle and it got one, the so-called 'Miracle of the Marne' which was arguably as much a result of German errors as French ability. First of all, German intelligence lost all track of the position of the 100,000 strong British Expeditionary Force which was to play a crucial role in the Battle of the Marne. Then, two subordinate German generals failed to adhere strictly to the Schlieffen Plan by swinging to the east of Paris rather than to the west. This blunder resulted in the nervous collapse of the German Commander-in-Chief who had just had to send two army corps eastward because of the sudden arrival of the Russians in East Prussia. Faithful to their promise to the French government, the Russians had put two armies into the field just 14 days after mobilisation (much sooner than the Germans expected). Military historians have generally agreed on the crucial importance of Russian intervention in saving France from collapse in 1914. Russia's intervention then gave France the chance to save herself, but she still needed the cool nerve of her Commander-in-Chief Joffre, a dogged pragmatist who had come up through the ranks via the unglamorous engineering corps. Joffre it was who realised the crucial importance of the railway system around Paris (which fortunately remained in French hands) and used it to transfer troops rapidly to pressure points along the Front. He even resorted to the expedient of rushing reinforcements to the Front in taxi-cabs - the famous 'Taxi-cabs of the Marne'. The contrast between Joffre's steadiness and the behaviour of his German counterpart von Moltke is obvious (the German Commander lacked the iron nerve that his famous uncle had shown in the Franco-Prussian war of 1870-1).

The Battle of the Marne is generally regarded as one of the decisive battles of the First World War because it ensured that the Schlieffen Plan failed, and that France was not knocked out of the war in six weeks. The German army was then forced to retire to the line of the River Aisne where it remained, more or less, for the next three and a half years. However, it has to be recognised that Germany had still won a partial victory because she remained in occupation of the whole of Belgium (bar a coastal strip around Ypres) and much of north-eastern France. The Germans were also left in possession of the more defensible higher ground, a crucial factor in the years to come.

In other respects too, France paid a terrible price for staving off total defeat in 1914. For predictably Plan 17 with its almost insane belief in victory achieved at the point of the bayonet, was a disaster. French armies advanced headlong into Alsace-Lorraine (in the blue tunics and red trousers which the High Command had recklessly refused to abandon in favour of a more sensible khaki). There the Germans, who had anticipated the direction of the French attack, waited for them and hundreds of thousands were mown down by artillery and machine guns.

By the end of 1914 the French army had already suffered a million casualties.

Why were the losses so heavy? It could be argued that the most significant factor was the High Command's resolute refusal to study earlier wars (such as the American Civil War of 1861-5 and the Russo-Japanese War of 1904-5) which showed that frontal assaults by infantry, and still more so by cavalry, were no match for machine guns and massed artillery. However, in their defence it should be remembered that the generals of the other belligerent powers made exactly the same mistake.

One French historian, Pierre Goubert, has argued that the French High Command was taken by surprise by the Schlieffen Plan, but this seems highly unlikely. It is more credible that they were taken aback by the speed of the German advance through Belgium, for strong points like Liége were expected to hold out much longer than they did.

The significance of the 1914 campaign was that both sides failed in their objectives. Both France (and one can add Britain) and Germany expected a quick victory. Both were proved wrong, but the French High Command, wedded as it was to an ultra-attacking doctrine, had special problems adapting to the new conditions. These new conditions were the existence of unbroken lines of trenches from the Channel coastline to the Swiss frontier. Attacking failure in 1914 had led to defensive stalemate on the western front.

One tantalising question remains. Could the Anglo-French side have exploited the victory on the Marne by following it up more rapidly? It seems unlikely. The Anglo-French troops were too exhausted after the Battle of the Marne, and the line of the Aisne was easily defended. The Germans had discovered that the shovel was a war-winning weapon.

4 Stalemate

The French Commander-in-Chief Joffre ordered a great offensive against the Germans in Champagne in December 1914. It got nowhere and was followed by another, equally futile one, in January 1915. Others followed in February and March 1915, again to no avail. In Artois, later in 1915, more effective use was made of artillery on a wider front, but the Germans used the heights of Vimy ridge to throw back the Allied assaults. Renewed attacks there in the autumn of 1915 were again bloodily repulsed. Little wonder then that the French called 1915 *L'Année Stérile* (the sterile year). By the end of it France had lost a further 400,000 killed and wounded. Yet still Joffre and his generals remained convinced that the war could be won by their armies on the western front.

The strategic and tactical stalemate on the western front inflicted dreadful suffering on the French army. It was a war of machine guns, barbed wire, futile frontal assaults on trenches, of rats, lice and a sodden mud-filled existence. Of the Champagne offensives a French soldier (the men acquired the nickname of the poilus or unshaven ones) wrote:

1 On the front of the Souain ridge were corpses of soldiers mown down by machine-gun in September 1915; they lay stretched out, face down, lined up as if on manoeuvre. The rain fell on them inexorably, bullets snapped their whitened bones. One night
5 Jacques, on patrol, saw enormous rats running off from under their faded caps, fat with human meat. He crawled towards the corpse, his heart beating loud; the helmet had rolled off, there was a grinning head with no flesh left on it, the skull bare, the eyes eaten up. Part of the false teeth had slipped out onto the rotting shirt and
10 some vile animal jumped out of the gaping mouth.

Such suffering meant that the poilu of December 1915 was a very different man from that of August 1914. Indifferent officers, poor food, inadequate leave, atrocious living conditions, all had their long-term impact on the rank and file troops who no longer shared their generals' almost religious fervour for offensives. Instead there was a solid patriotism, a fatalistic attitude towards the wretched conditions in which the soldiers lived, and more sympathy for ordinary German soldiers who suffered in the same way than for French generals who lived in luxurious conditions far behind the front line.

The stalemate in the West encouraged politicians in France and Britain to seek other means of winning the war quickly. One option, which was never popular with Joffre and the French military, was the 'eastern' strategy. This involved sending an Allied expedition to seize the Black Sea Straits and Constantinople, which would knock Turkey out of the war, and link up with France's ally Russia. But Joffre and his colleagues remained convinced that the war would have to be won on the western front.

Nevertheless, an Anglo-French plan was formulated to seize the Straits from the Turks and advance on Constantinople. It was one in which France's contribution was in a minor key (she sent 79,000 men, compared with 410,000 from the British Empire) but she lost ships and men in this (initially) promising attempt to win the war away from the carnage on the western front. The Gallipoli campaign has been described as the 'great if' of the war because if it had succeeded there was a prospect of decisive victory in the east. But military bungling meant that the essentials of surprise and secrecy were lost (an Allied naval attack signalled the landing that was to follow), and the Turks were given time to prepare their defences.

5 Verdun

In 1916 it was the Germans who took the initiative on the western front by instigating the massive battle for the French fortress town of Verdun. The new German Commander-in-Chief, von Falkenhayn, believed that the war could only be won on the western front, and his strategy was to 'bleed France white' by sucking her military reserves into a huge set-piece battle for Verdun. Falkenhayn reasoned that France would not be able to entertain the idea of losing such an ancient and symbolically important town. In this at least he was correct.

There is no doubt that at the outset of the battle for Verdun the French were taken by surprise. Otherwise they would not have removed all the heavy guns protecting the forts around Verdun and placed them in the front line. This, and the violence of the German assault, accounted for early setbacks (on the first day of the battle of Verdun, the Germans fired a million shells).

A crucial decision was then made by Joffre on 25 February to appoint Philippe Pétain as Commander of the Verdun sector. Described by one historian as cold and methodical with the taciturn nature of a northerner, Pétain was a complete contrast to the devotees of the 'spirit' and 'guts' school of Foch and even Joffre himself. By training he was an infantry man, and by temperament a defensive fighter who was niggardly with the lives of his men (a rare quality in a First World War general on either side). Pétain's motto was *Courage; on les aura* (Courage; we shall have them). It was he who reorganised the defence of Verdun, and built the 'Sacred Way' *(Voie sacrée)* along which 5,000 supply lorries rumbled every day as the Germans had captured the railway system around Verdun. His constant rotation of troops in the Verdun sector kept up the morale of its defenders because no one soldier spent excessive time in the front line there.

Yet the stereotype of heroic and united resistance is partly misleading. As one historian has pointed out, even Pétain despaired in June 1916 when a heavy German assault was drenching Verdun with phosgene gas shells. He told Joffre that the city would fall. But the doughty Commander-in-Chief refused to concede defeat and when challenged about the gravity of this decision for the French army, retorted, 'I've taken plenty of others'. In the end the French were victorious at Verdun, but the cost was a terrible price of 350,000 lives.

Was it a price worth paying? This question has taxed military historians ever since, and some have argued that the French army should have cut its losses and evacuated Verdun in February 1916, for its loss would not have forced France out of the war. It remains true, however, that the German failure to 'bleed France white' at Verdun cost them equally dearly, and that the French defence of the fortress town prevented a decisive enemy breakthrough.

But the French obsession with Verdun may have crucially affected the outcome of the Battle of the Somme which began in July 1916. The Battle for Verdun meant that only 14 French divisions were available to fight on the Somme instead of the planned 40. So the cost of victory there may have been prohibitive in the context of the whole war.

The long-term effects of the Battle of Verdun were considerable. The French army was exhausted by its massive exertions in that battle which left a shattering psychological legacy. A French lieutenant wrote after the battle that: 'They will not be able to make us do it again another day: that would be to misconstrue the price of our effort. They will have to resort to those who have not lived out these days.' Some historians have seen in the carnage at Verdun the genesis of France's catastrophic defeat in 1940 when her supposedly powerful army was defeated in only six weeks. The soldiers of 1940, they allege, were unwilling to repeat the self-sacrifice of 1916.

6 Nivelle's Offensive

In April 1917 the French army launched a great offensive in the west, but it brought about only a 4-mile advance in 10 days on a 16-mile front, during which 28,000 prisoners were taken. The man responsible for this offensive was General Robert Nivelle, the new Commander-in-Chief who like Pétain, was a hero of the fighting at Verdun. But there any resemblance between the two men ended. Nivelle was confident - fatally overconfident as it turned out - that offensive spirit could win the war. He also had a charm which bewitched politicians, and he could speak English well, a talent which allowed him to win over the British Prime Minister Lloyd George to the idea of a great new offensive. The British agreed to mount a subsidiary attack.

A number of things went wrong even before the attack started. Hearing stories about the impending offensive (amazingly the French published information about it in their own newspapers!), the Germans evacuated their front-line positions and retreated to strong points up to 40 kilometres behind them. Left behind was a flooded area which could easily be dominated by German artillery.

In February 1917 revolution broke out in Russia causing disruption which made it impossible for France's ally to launch a supporting offensive in the east. These facts made Nivelle's colleagues, especially Pétain, uneasy, but the Commander-in-Chief remained supremely confident saying that a surprise attack could break through the German lines in 24 or 48 hours. But the element of surprise had already been lost and it would have been hard to preserve secrecy when 50 divisions and 50,000 guns were to be used in the offensive.

The way that Nivelle 'talked up' the offensive merely inflated expectations of victory to a dangerous degree. Nothing less than a decisive breakthrough would do, but Nivelle himself had been forced to agree that he would call off the offensive if it had not attained its objectives within three days (a promise he failed to keep). To make matters even worse, the Germans had captured a copy of Nivelle's plan in early April.

Whereas historians have regarded Verdun as an example of heroic defence, they have generally regarded Nivelle's offensive as an ill-planned disaster. But this view has been challenged by the British historian John Terraine who has pointed out that when compared with the carnage which resulted from Joffre's 1915 offensives (let alone Verdun), Nivelle's achievement was considerable. This view was backed up just after the war by the British Official History of the War which stated that if the Germans had achieved as much as Nivelle, 'they would have broadcast the battle to the world as a colossal victory'. Nevertheless, Nivelle was sacked as Commander-in-Chief because he had not provided the promised decisive victory. His failure was a failure to meet the aspirations of the poilus, who had been fed propaganda about how the Nivelle offensive would make the longed-for break-through. Having been promised the earth, their disillusionment, when it came, was all the greater.

7 The Mutinies

Between April and June 1917 the French army was paralysed by a series of mutinies by front-line troops. By early June only two divisions on the central front (which covered Paris) could be relied on. The poilus would hold the line, but they would undertake no more pointless frontal assaults against nests of German machine guns. An officer wrote: This passivity was a direct result of the failure of Nivelle's offensive.

All the companies are in a state of turmoil; the men are receiving letters from friends informing them of the present spirit and urging them not to march; the ringleaders are becoming insolent, others are trying to influence their comrades.

This was Pétain's moment - he was brought in as Commander-in-Chief to replace the disgraced Nivelle. Above all the other generals in the First World War he cared about the welfare of the average soldier in the trenches, and his men knew it. Now at last the poilus were given better pay and conditions with the result that morale was restored, but death sentences were passed on the 55 ringleaders of the mutiny in order to reimpose discipline.

However, the French army was never the same again. It had endured Verdun in 1916 but the failure of the Nivelle offensive in 1917 had broken its offensive spirit. Pétain realised that it could no longer win the war on its own, and his strategy was to await the coming of large numbers of American reinforcements after the USA's entry into the war in April 1917 on the Anglo-French side. Verdun, Nivelle's offensive, the mutinies; these three crises were inextricably linked.

Verdun had demonstrated the capacity of the French army to absorb punishment and for defence; Nivelle's failure had shown that it could not win the war on its own; and the mutinies had shown that there were limits even to the poilus' endurance, and that the strain on the Western front would have to be borne by the British, at least until the Americans could arrive in significant numbers.

8 Politicians and the War

France had gone to war united. This unity was personified by the 'sacred union' government of 1914. However, as the heady days of national unity in August 1914 receded into the background, tensions emerged in the French government.

One important issue was civil-military relations. Who was to run the war, the civilians or the military? In the opening phase of the war, after his victory on the Marne, Joffre was virtually above criticism. But his political bosses were not, and the 'sacred union' government of Viviani was forced to resign in October 1915 as a result of alleged mismanagement of the war. This was a way of expressing dissatisfaction with the fact that Joffre's offensives in 1915 had failed, because at that stage Parliament dared not remove Joffre himself.

Another factor in Viviani's overthrow had been accusations of pro-clericalism against the Prime Minister in favouring the promotion of right-wing Catholic officers (religious disputes had plagued French politics before the war). So Briand, his successor as Prime Minister, included two strong anti-clericals in his Cabinet to assure Republicans that there would be no undue Catholic influence in the government. This counter-balance was needed because there were high-ranking officers in the army leadership who were strongly Catholic and actually in favour of restoring the monarchy.

Briand also wanted to assert civilian control over the conduct of the war, and was instrumental in securing the eventual dismissal of Joffre at the end of 1916, after the carnage at Verdun. Briand himself then fell from power in March 1917 after making a disastrously unpopular appointment of a defence minister. He was succeeded by Ribot.

In April 1917 a meeting was held at Compiègne between France's generals and politicians. Ribot seems to have been seduced by Nivelle's argument for a knockout blow in the West, to the extent of ignoring criticisms of other generals and refusing Nivelle's offer to resign as Commander-in-Chief. In this instance, the promise of victory seems to have displaced the Prime Minister's own sense of realism about what was possible (by contrast, the British Prime Minister, Lloyd George, remained deeply suspicious of his own Commander-in-Chief). As described above, Nivelle's attack went ahead with disastrous con-sequences for the army.

Among the political spin-offs of Nivelle's failure was a surge of defeatism among some French politicians. It was the alleged failure of the government to control a group of pacifists associated with the newspaper *Le Bonnet Rouge* (the Red Bonnet) in August 1917 that forced Ribot's resignation.

The precarious military situation also played its part in bringing down Ribot's successor Painlevé who survived only two months before his ministry was forced to resign because of accusations that it was secretly negotiating for peace with Germany. The accusation was false but it demonstrated the uncertainty that surrounded France's military and political future in 1917.

9 Clemenceau

The main instigator of the fall of the Ribot and Painlevé governments was Georges Clemenceau, a veteran of Third Republic politics who was nicknamed 'the Tiger'. Everything about Clemenceau was colourful. He was accused of being an English spy before the war, he married a woman 30 years younger than himself, and he aroused such hatred among political opponents that their campaigns were based on the slogan 'Death to Clemenceau'!

Once in power, Clemenceau did little to appease his political opponents. He dominated the government, appointed a nonentity as Foreign Minister, and seemed contemptuous of the concept of the 'sacred union' which had united France at the beginning of the war. The Socialists alleged that they were treated as enemies of the state. But Clemenceau was not the sort of man who was likely to be intimidated by the crisis of confidence facing France in the autumn of 1917. Months after becoming Prime Minister, he was to tell Parliament: 'Internal policy, I wage war; foreign policy, I still wage war.' There was never any doubt about his commitment to victory over Germany. Everything about him was tigerish.

In an apparently deliberate attempt to intimidate defeatists, Clemenceau ordered the execution of the notorious German spy Mata Hari (some recent research suggests that she may not have been a spy at all). More significantly, he dismissed the former Finance Minister Caillaux who had been openly campaigning for peace. Such actions fed the left-wing view that the Prime Minister, a member of the centre-left Radical Party, set up a repressive and even dictatorial regime until the war ended in November 1918.

However, Clemenceau's biographer points out that he was not as tough in office as some of his uncompromising talk in opposition might have suggested he would be. The case against Mata Hari was in fact underway before Clemenceau became Prime Minister, and he proved unexpectedly mild in his dealings with trade unionists whom he had brutally intimidated before the war. Employers were actually encouraged to make concessions to the trade unionists' demands for higher wages. Such evidence inclines the historian J.F. MacMillan to conclude that, 'As for being a dictator, Clemenceau was able to govern as he did only because he enjoyed the support of the great majority of the French people, who shared his commitment to outright victory.'

Precisely because of the totality of his commitment to the war effort and because he had forced opponents out of office by accusing them of favouring a separate peace between France and the enemy powers, Clemenceau could not be associated with any sort of peace feeler. A suggestion, therefore, by the Austro-Hungarian Foreign Minister that France had secretly been in touch with him about peace talks was ferociously denied. Clemenceau's denials about secret talks seem convincing given everything that is known about his vehement patriotism. The ultimate issue for him though was how and when the war was to be won.

1 I would propose to invite our Permanent Military Advisers in their examination of the problem, not to forget that the War has become largely one of exhaustion. It may be that victory will be achieved by endurance rather than by a military decision. Russia has already 5 collapsed, at any rate, for the present, but it must be remembered that Turkey and Austria are neither of them very far from collapse.

The final objective now, as formerly, is the overthrow of Prussian militarism, but I would ask the Permanent Military advisers to weigh carefully whether possibly that object may not be 10 brought nearer final achievement by the overthrow, first of all of Germany's allies, and the isolation of Germany; whether in fact the final overthrow of Germany may not be best reserved until the forces of the Allies, greatly augmented by a fully matured American Army can be focused and concentrated as a climax to the 15 War on this final objective.

In this context, Clemenceau had one supreme achievement. He ended the wrangling between the civilians and the military about who was to run the war, which had rumbled on since its start. He may have been fortunate that neither Pétain nor Foch wanted to be supreme warlords like their counterparts in Germany, but no general challenged 'the Tiger's' authority and there was no utopian masterplan for winning the war like Nivelle's.

10 The Home Front

French public opinion was not prepared for a long war, and even when it had been raging for some time bizarre delusions about it continued. One contemporary representation of trench warfare showed rooms behind the trenches with billiard tables, a restaurant and bathrooms! French soldiers also received letters from well-meaning old ladies with questions like, 'But when it's raining you surely don't fight?' and 'Is there any fighting on Sundays?' Historians have remarked on how such ignorance led to estrangement and bitterness between the soldiers and civilians. Foreigners certainly remarked on the normalcy of life in Paris which was only a few kilometres from the front line.

Some parts of French society also seemed to be benefiting from the war. Extra allowances for soldiers' families, for example, meant that some peasant families were better off than in peacetime. Even industrial workers, whose wages were not increased, were assisted by the government freeze on household rents.

But ignorance about what was going on in the war was largely a result of rigid censorship which exaggerated tiny local successes and 'Boche' (the slang word for the Germans) atrocities. This was designed to keep up morale but such *bourrage de crâne* (eyewash) succeeded only in alienating the poilus and (by the end of the war) civilians as well. Historians have commented on the good fortune of successive French governments that the mutinies of 1917 did not coincide with the profound civilian war weariness evident early in 1918, by which time Pétain had patched up French army morale.

11 The Economic Effort

Total war faced the French government, which was wedded to free market economics, with a dilemma. How much government intervention was needed in the running of the war effort? At first, the government was reluctant to intervene at all in the war economy and relied on co-operation with great corporations like Creusot, but by 1916 this policy was proven to be inadequate. France was, after all, fighting the sort of war in which a million shells could be fired in a day, and by 1918 the state was intervening in the economy in a way which would have been unimaginable in 1914.

In 1916 consortia had been created to organise different industries more efficiently with employers sitting on government-run committees. In 1917 measures were taken to control prices, and in the following year, rationing was introduced for commodities such as bread and sugar. Control of the war economy had by then passed into the hands of small teams of ministers and advisers. The most notable figures were Clementel, who was in charge of the mobilisation of the industrial workforce, and Albert Thomas, a Socialist who was Minister of Munitions until 1917. As the table indicates, the achievement of French industrial mobilisation was considerable.

Numbers employed by the French armaments industry 1918

Civilian Male Workers	425,000
Men	497,000 (subject to military discipline)
Women	430,000
Children under 18	133,000
Foreign workers	108,000
Colonials	60,000
Prisoners of War	40,000
Mutilés (wounded or disabled)	13,000
Total	1.7 million

One estimate suggests that French wartime production was increased by 50 per cent through the use of Taylorist techniques (Taylor was the American inventor of mass production conveyor belt techniques). However, in some respects this was only an extension of pre-war achievement, for before 1914 the French motor industry had already become Europe's largest producer. The presence of up to half a million women in the workforce was also a significant consequence of the coming of war. In 1917 they reflected war weariness in the country by striking both in munitions factories and (the more unlikely) Parisian dress shops.

Was war a social catalyst as far as women were concerned? Seemingly not, in that women were soon forced back into the kitchen when the war was over (unlike in Britain, they did not get the vote). But women did have a high profile in the pacifist rumblings in France in 1917, and Louise Saumoneau was a notable anti-war Socialist who had links with like-minded Socialists abroad.

By contrast, the wave of male workers' strikes in 1918 were inspired by the Bolshevik Revolution in Russia, whereas those by female workers had been about poor pay, bad conditions and ending the war rather than bringing about revolution. Given the appalling losses in the war, the wonder is that France's social fabric held together as well as it did, and the economic achievement between 1914 and 1918 was formidable. Despite the loss of her valuable northern departments, France had re-equipped the Serbian Army, provided the British with thousands of aircraft and railway engines, and armed the Americans despite the burden imposed on her by having to maintain her own huge army. All the pre-war political tensions between Right and Left did not disappear in wartime, but the Third Republic was able to sustain the burden of total war which demanded the mobilisation of the entire population. In doing so it managed to avoid falling under the sort of military dictatorship that existed in Germany from 1916 onwards.

12 Victory

In the winter of 1917-18 no-one in France would have suspected that victory was on the horizon. The Italians, who had joined the Entente side in 1915, were catastrophically defeated at Caporetto in October 1917, and had to be rescued from disaster by Anglo-French reinforcements. More seriously, Russia fell under Bolshevik rule in November 1917 and ceased to make any meaningful contribution to the Allied war effort. Her formal departure from the war was signalled by the Treaty of Brest Litovsk (March 1918). Thereafter French generals were haunted by one question. Would the Germans be able to make a decisive breakthrough on the western front with troops transferred from the East (although it tends to be forgotten that German distrust of Bolshevik motives meant that some German units were kept in the East). The failure of Allied offensives in the West in 1917 meant that there was little that the Anglo-French side could do other than await American reinforcements. Russia's collapse now meant that there was a window of opportunity for Germany and her allies.

On 21 March 1918 the Germans launched their Kaiserschlacht (Emperor's Battle), although strangely it was the doughty British rather than the war-weary French who were targeted. A massive attack around Saint Quentin broke through the British lines and the Allies were faced with a crisis. Pétain's reaction to this was to husband his resources, and he was reluctant to send reinforcements to aid his British ally. This in turn made the British consider a retreat to the Channel ports and the evacuation of their army (something they did do in 1940). Again Paris was threatened by the German army.

This was the moment when Foch redeemed his error of being over-enthusiastic about the power of the offensive in 1914. An inter-Allied Conference was held on 26 March and it was Foch's optimistic spirit which prevailed rather than Pétain's pessimism. As the German advance was edging towards the vital railway junction of Amiens, Foch told the Allied representatives: 'I shall fight in front of Amiens, I shall fight in Amiens itself, and I shall fight behind Amiens.' He created sufficient impression to be appointed co-ordinator of the Allied armies (although the Americans obstinately insisted on fighting as a separate force). Foch's capacity as Supreme Commander was to be tested to the limit, although he was probably assisted by what military historians have seen as a serious German blunder in attacking the British first.

Only in May did the Germans finally attack the French on the Chemins des Dames in Champagne, in what was meant to be a diversionary operation, but to their surprise, the French line buckled between the strong points of Soissons and Rheims, and a sizeable breakthrough was made. The French had been sending reinforcements to other parts of the front, and this offers a partial explanation for the reverse. By 30 May the Germans had once again reached the River

Marne, and Pétain was prepared to order a general retreat (he was still Commander-in-Chief of the French Army under Foch's overall command). But the German Commander-in-Chief, von Ludendorff, had now shot his bolt, lacking the reserves to make further offensives of such weight. When a last one was tried in July the French, already forewarned by prisoners, turned the tables in 1917-style by retiring to prepared second-line positions where they held the German advance.

After this the Allies were able to go over to the offensive. The German spring and summer offensives had cost both sides a million casualties. As military historians have pointed out, for the Germans these losses were absolute - they could not be made good - while on the other side, the Allies were being reinforced by the Americans to the tune of a quarter of a million men each month. By August, there were a million of them in France, and they became, in Ludendorff's words, 'the deciding factor in the war'. Fittingly, however, it was the British Tommy and the French poilu who won the decisive battle around Amiens on 8 August. Ludendorff described this battle (in which tanks played a crucial role) as the 'black day of the German army'.

Then despite desperate German defence in the autumn of 1918, the Allies pushed remorselessly on, and Germany's allies began to collapse. The French striking up through Greece from Salonica knocked Bulgaria out of the war, and the British did the same to the Turks. Austria-Hungary collapsed in October, and the German generals had already advised the Kaiser to sue for peace.

13 Peace

Peace duly arrived on 11 November 1918 when a ceasefire came into operation on the western front. France was left with the problem of what to do with its victory. For even when the war was raging, French war aims had little coherent shape. Alsace-Lorraine would, of course, have to be restored to France, but otherwise there was confusion. The French Right wanted to break Germany up and restore her to her pre-1870 disunity, while the colonial lobby wanted to make acquisitions from the German empire in Africa and the Turkish one in the Middle East. The Foreign Office (Quai d'Orsay) was concerned about the loss of massive French investment to Bolshevik Russia, and supported intervention there. Only on the terrible price of victory would there have been general agreement.

14 Conclusion

What was the significance of the First World War in the history of the Third Republic? First, it demonstrated the essential patriotism of the French nation which battled on despite appalling setbacks to ultimate victory. Second, the achievement of victory marked a real watershed, in that mobilisation of the people for war involved an unprecedented degree of state intervention in the economy. Third, and despite reservations about Clemenceau's behaviour, the wartime experience showed the essential soundness of France's democratic institutions. She did not become a military dictatorship like Germany, and neither did she fall victim to apparent Bolshevik influence during the last winter of the war.

For all that experience of the war was a shattering one, and its shadow lay across the whole inter-war period.

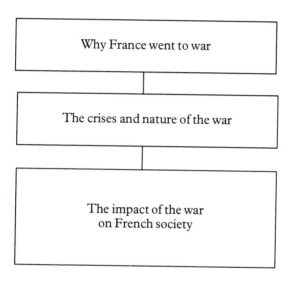

Summary - War and Peace, 1914-18

Making notes on *'War and Peace 1914-18'*

When making your notes on this chapter you should have three questions under consideration: i) Why did France go to war in 1914? ii) What were the major turning points and crises in the war as far as France was concerned? iii) What were the socio-economic effects of the war on France?

However, most students are likely, in the first instance, to need to follow the chronological structure of the chapter in their notetaking. Once this has been done, the three broader issues above can be addressed.

The following headings and sub-headings may be appropriate.
1   The Outbreak of War.
1.1 France's role in the July crisis.
1.2 French war planning.
1.3 The Battle of the Marne and its consequences.
2   Stalemate in the West.
2.1 The technology of stalemate.
2.2 Gallipoli; failure in the east.
3   Three Crises.
3.1 Verdun.
3.2 Nivelle's offensive.
3.3 The mutinies.
4   The Domestic Front.
4.1 The role of politicians.
4.2 Social and economic effects of the war.
5   Crisis and Victory.
5.1 The German offensive 1918.
5.2 Foch and the Allied victory.
5.3 Did France achieve her war aims?

Answering essay questions on 'War and Peace 1914-18'

The focus of some essay questions in this chapter will be on military history and some students find this topic offputting. But the sweep of the questions is broad and does not require you to be a military buff. A sound knowledge of the broad sweep of events during the war rather than the intricacies of military tactics is what is required. Study the following questions:

1   Assess French responsibility for the outbreak of the First World War.
2   Why did French hopes for victory in 1914 prove to be an illusion?
3   'The price paid for victory at Verdun was too high.' Discuss.
4   What were the major economic and social affects of the war on French society?

Many students would find Question 1 the most difficult here because it demands knowledge of the role played by the other powers in the July Crisis, and will require you to use other books in the Access Series as well as this one. Question 3 may also prove to be something of a trap because some candidates when presented with a quotation merely succumb to the temptation to agree with it! The examiner will want to see that you are aware that there is another side to this particular coin. Yes, the price paid for victory was high, but it can be argued that France had to win at Verdun.

Source-based questions on 'War and Peace 1914-18'

1 The Poilu's Perspective of the War

Carefully read the extracts on pages 16 and 22. Answer the following questions.

a) What do you understand by the phrase 'lined up as if on manoeuvre (page 16) (1 mark)

b) How are the horrors of trench warfare made clear in the first extract? (6 marks)

c) Use the material in the first extract, and any other material in the chapter to explain the events referred to in the second extract. (8 marks)

2 Clemenceau's First Address to the Supreme Allied Council, November 1917.

Carefully read the extract on page 22. Answer the following questions.

a) Use the material available in chapter 2 to show that by the time Clemenceau was speaking the war had indeed become 'largely one of exhaustion'. (7 marks)

b) What strategy does Clemenceau suggest should be followed in the second paragraph, and how successful was it? (8 marks)

CHAPTER 3

The Cost of Victory: Reconstruction and Economic Crisis 1918-39

If France in 1918 was France triumphant, she was also France devastated. This devastation was human, material and financial. Of all the belligerent powers, France lost a higher proportion of men (Serbia excepted) in the First World War than anyone else. In all nearly 17 per cent of the French men mobilised in 1914 were killed in the war, and a generation of young men died in the trenches. The glory of 1918 was, therefore, purchased at a hideous price.

France - The Cost of the First World War	
Killed	1,322,000
Wounded	3,000,000
Permanently Disabled	167,000
Widows Eligible for Pensions	600,000
Orphans	750,000

What was the effect of such losses? One historian has written of how the trauma of the war persisted throughout the inter-war period.

> 1 Countless others would suffer recurrent nervous disorders induced
>   by the abiding effects of shell shock. Once again it is beyond the
>   powers of the historian to recapture the physical and moral
>   suffering experienced by *mutilés*, wounded or disabled ones and
> 5 their families; but one does not doubt that it was immense.

The sheer human loss would mean that throughout the post-war period France was to be chronically short of labour (even in 1938 there was only half the normal number of 19-21 year olds). This shortfall could be made up by bringing in immigrant labour from Poland, Spain, Italy and Belgium (even if this created social tensions with French workers). But it could not outweigh the other stark reality facing successive French governments. This was that France, even though she had been victorious over Germany, would be in the situation in 1940 of 41 million French facing 69 million Germans. This bleak demographic fact was to dominate French foreign policy between the wars - and much of domestic policy as well. For how could a devastated and numerically inferior France keep her neighbour in check, particularly as that neighbour also had superior resources of coal, steel and chemicals? Even the survivors of the great conflict had their impact on France's domestic and foreign policies. These surviving servicemen were often embittered by their experiences which made many of them into life-long paupers because of their disabilities. Three and a half million of them were to join ex-servicemen's organisations which, with their fear of another war, were a potent influence on French government policy.

1 Reparations and Reconstruction

The material damage to France's northern departments was also catastrophic. Mines were destroyed, railway lines wrecked and millions of hectares of agricultural land ruined. Much of this damage was deliberately inflicted by retreating Germans in 1918. Two examples will serve to underline the extent of the material and physical devastation. In 1914 Soissons had 18,000 inhabitants. In 1918 it had just 500. In Rheims people were reduced to living in caves to avoid the persistent artillery bombardments. Reconstruction was to be a major burden for the French economy.

The traditional view that the French unreasonably expected Germany to foot the bill for the damage done in her northern departments, has now largely been discounted. At the outset the French commerce minister Clémentel proposed that the inter-Allied economic co-operation of the war years should be continued, but with defeated Germany fully integrated into the new system. Unless this were done Clémentel feared that German industrial might would threaten French again in the future. But if Germany were fully integrated into the new system her industrial resources could be used to benefit the global economy. Neither was there any suggestion from the French at this stage that Germany should be crippled by severe reparations.

Disappointingly for France this imaginative initiative by Clémentel was turned down by the Americans, who were not ready for this sort of peacetime co-operation, but even then the French demand for reparations was pitched at the relatively modest level of 120 milliard gold marks. They wanted to retain the support of US President Woodrow Wilson, who favoured lenient treatment of Germany, and it was the British who demanded a much higher figure which would include compensation for material damage (the ultimate reparations figure of 6.5 billion gold marks was fixed only in 1921 - the Versailles Treaty did not mention a specific figure).

Only then were French governments fully committed to the principle of *la Boche paiera* (the German will pay) and the expectation that German money would pay for the reconstruction of France's ruined northern departments.

This expectation, the historian Anthony Adamthwaite has argued, was partly a result of serious domestic financial weakness. France did not have a proper system of direct taxation like Britain and the USA, and no income tax at all until 1920. This had meant that of 55 milliard francs borrowed by French governments to pay for the First World War, only seven milliards had been raised by taxation.

So in 1919, after the failure of the Clémentel initiative, the French government was faced with some unpalatable facts. Either the Germans would have to pay for the whole cost of reconstruction, or the French would have to reform their tax system and increase taxation on the wealthy (something French governments were to prove notoriously reluctant to do in the 1920s). They suspected in any case that German complaints about the level of reparations was exaggerated (another modern historian has pointed out that the amount fixed in 1921 was still only about 6 per cent of Germany's Gross National Product). This made them even less inclined to come to terms with economic reality, the fact that reconstruction could not be funded entirely out of German payments. In the first place because the Germans were obstructive about paying (provoking an armed French occupation of the Ruhr industrial area in 1923, see page 58), and in the second because the United States did France no favours either. France owed her large sums of money which had been borrowed to pay for her war effort, but when in 1923 the French government asked for some of this debt to be written off, the US President Coolidge replied tersely, 'they hired the money didn't they?'

Were French expectations unreasonable? Perhaps, but not surprising in the light of their sufferings in the First World War. Was France malicious in her demands on a defeated foe as the traditional historical view suggests? The evidence of the Clémentel initiative suggests otherwise, as does the economic argument about the relatively low level of reparations compared with Germany's total production capacity.

Where we can perhaps be critical of French reparations policy is in its unbudging assumption that reconstruction would be funded by the Germans and the refusal to acknowledge that it could not be. This, as Foreign Minister Briand later recognised, caused serious economic difficulties, because French governments consistently overspent on reconstruction assuming that reparations payments would then balance the budget. They felt, rightly or wrongly, that natural justice dictated that Germany should pay for the damage her armies had done.

2 Post-war Politics

Wartime politics in France had been dominated, from 1917 onwards, by the combative figure of Georges Clemenceau, 'The Tiger' who had led the country from apparent disaster to the victory of 1918. As Prime Minister, Clemenceau called parliamentary elections for November 1919, and used his influence as *père-la-victoire* (father of victory) to secure a massive electoral victory for the right wing Bloc National. The 'Block', actually a coalition of centre and right-wing parties, won 400 out of 616 seats in the Chamber of Deputies, even if the swing in public opinion was relatively small.

a) Clemenceau's Fall

Clemenceau expected the nation to show its gratitude by duly electing him President of the Republic, for which post he stood in 1920 (the President was elected by members of the Chamber of Deputies). To the surprise of many, however, Clemenceau was defeated by a nonentity, Paul Deschanel, whose main claim to fame is that on one occasion he fell out of the Presidential train in his pyjamas, and had some difficulty in convincing the local police that he was indeed who he claimed to be, the President of the Republic! He later went mad.

Why was Clemenceau defeated in such a humiliating fashion? His defeat seems to have been due, in part, to a fear that he would weaken Parliament and strengthen the presidency. The nationalist right also accused Clemenceau of not punishing Germany severely enough at Versailles. Most important though seems to have been the fact that the ultra conservative Chamber of 1919, *l'horizon bleu* (sky blue) Chamber had more practising Catholics in it than any since 1876, and Clemenceau was a noted anti-clerical. He would certainly not have approved of the ceremonial canonisation of Joan of Arc in 1920, attended by a large number of right-wing parliamentarians, or the resumption of diplomatic ties with the Vatican brought about by the National Block.

Did Clemenceau's defeat make any difference to the fate of post-war France? Perhaps not, as (religion apart) the policies pursued were not markedly different from those he might have supported, but his fall showed that politicians appeared to prefer having a nonentity for President rather than a figure of substance. Clemenceau was not to be the last major figure in French politics between the wars to be rejected in this way.

3 The Split on the Left

In October 1917 the Bolshevik Party seized power in Russia, so ending the involvement of France's main ally in the First World War, and establishing a communist regime in that country. This had immediate ramifications in France where part of the working class and trade union movement seemed to favour a revolutionary solution to France's problems on the Russia model.

This split became formalised at the Congress of the French Socialist Party at Tours in December 1920. Part of the party broke away and joined the Communist Third International (controlled from Moscow) taking with it the control of the party newspaper. This section formed the PCF (French Communist Party) while the remaining faction of the Socialist Party under Léon Blum remained faithful to the democratic ideals of the Republic. The Socialists were later to be in coalition with the bourgeois Radical Socialists, but dared not enter the government with the Radicals lest they drive the more left-wing Socialists into the arms of the Communists. This was an old issue for French socialism. Could a Socialist take part in a government with bourgeois parties? The existence of a new, even more left-wing party, the Communists, only made the choice more difficult.

The appearance of a genuine communist party in France in 1920 might have created a revolutionary situation. Even before the split on the Left, there had been a series of strikes by miners, metalworkers and railwaymen in 1919-20. These men, who were members of the Confederation Generale du Travail (General Confederation of Workers), were discontented with the moderate position of their union on workers' rights and pay and also objected strongly to Clemenceau's decision to intervene in arms against the Bolsheviks in Russia (communism was anathema to the old warrior). The result was that the trade union movement, like the political movement, split in two. The radicals became communists and set up their own Confederation Generale du Travail Unitaire (General Confederation of United Workers) in opposition to the old socialist CGT.

At the time there seemed to be a real chance of communist revolution in France itself, and historians have pondered about why no revolution took place. At the peak of the agitation against French involvement in Russia in April 1919, the Socialist Marty was able to instigate a mutiny in the French Black Sea Fleet, and this mutiny then spread subsequently to the great French naval bases at Brest and Toulon. A breakdown in discipline in the armed forces could have been the prelude to a radical revolution in France in 1919-20.

Yet it was not. Fortunately for the government, the army remained loyal, and Clemenceau showed his usual resolve in turning out a force of 17,000 men with tanks to crush the strikers at home while the Black Sea mutineers were also dealt with. The revolutionary crisis, if indeed there had ever been one, was over.

In the long run it was the formal split in the French Left which was to take on the most significance. The bad blood between the Socialists and the Communists, and their labour wings the CGT and CGTU made unity on the Left an impossibility between the wars. Only once, in 1936-7, was a government formed with Communist assistance and this proved to be shortlived.

4 Religion and Centralism

While the Socialists and Communists fought it out on the French Left, the strong Catholic bias of the National Block seemed likely to re-awaken the old pre-war struggle between clericals and anti-clericals. While the Block had campaigned with the bland slogan that 'secularization must be compatible with the liberties and rights of all citizens whatever their religion' it actually provoked trouble with the anti-clericals in the restored province of Alsace. There it refused to apply the law of 1905 separating Church and State (Alsace being at that time under German rule) so preserving the Church's dominant position.

This action predictably outraged the anti-clericals, who had fought such a bitter campaign before 1914 to end the Catholic Church's privileged position as the established Church in France. However, the issue in Alsace was as much to do with local autonomy as it was to do with religion, for between 1871 and 1914, when it was under German rule, Alsace had a good deal of autonomy which allowed it to use its own dialect in education and administration. France, by contrast, was a much more centralised state, and the government insisted on the use of the French language. This use of centralised power was resented by the Alsatians, and when the National Block lost the 1924 elections, a more sensitive policy of assimilation was adopted.

Alsace was not the only issue between the Church and its enemies, however. Anti-clericals (a group which included Communists, Socialists and Radicals) were suspicious of the Catholic revival in the 1920s and of new Catholic organisations like the National Catholic Federation, founded in 1924. These seemed to be extremely right wing in their politics, and some supporters of militant Catholicism later became fascists.

The Left was especially outraged by the Action Française movement and its influential leader, the intellectual Charles Maurras, which had strong links with the Church, and was noted for its ultra-nationalist opinions. So chauvinistic in fact was Action Française that Pope Pius XI became alarmed lest it prejudice improving Franco-German relations, and in 1926 he condemned it and its widely read newspaper.

This action, though laudable, did not prevent members of the clergy and laity supporting Action Française, or kill the suspicion on the Left that the Catholic Church was an ally of the far Right in France. Indeed, as the historian Christopher Andrew has pointed out, the crucial 1936 election in France, which returned the only united Left government of the inter-war period, seems to demonstrate the permanence of the old clerical-anti-clerical split in France. Catholics, Andrew notes, voted in overwhelming numbers for the Right and the anti-clericals voted in equally large numbers for the Left. This makes a point about the essential conservatism of voters in the Third Republic, but what does it tell us about the significance of religion as an issue between 1918 and 1939? Not much perhaps in that the 1930s did not see much evidence of struggle between Catholicism and the Left. Other historians argue that while religion was used as a political weapon by both Right and Left in the 1920s, it then became a smokescreen for social and political animosities in the 1930s. Using the label 'clerical' or 'anti-clerical' merely added to the lexicon of abuse, they claim, in the ideological struggle between Left and Right.

a) Poincaré and the Fall of the National Block

More significant in the 1920s than the religious issue was the economic crisis faced by France. Economic crisis was to be an ongoing feature of the inter-war period with the major issue being the relationship between tax reform and reparations.

The dominant figure in the National Block was Raymond Poincaré, a dour, humourless, fiercely anti-socialist lawyer who was to have the major role in managing the French economy in the crisis years between 1924 and 1926. He was regarded as the champion of the rentiers, that class of small businessmen and shopkeepers in France who relied a good deal on fixed income from investments and were increasingly alarmed by the growth of inflation. Poincaré shared their preoccupations as Prime Minister, and believed like them in the virtues of thrift and the capitalist system. By 1923, however, he was forced by France's economic weakness to consider introducing a package of tax increases which the Left had been demanding for some time. When the Senate, the upper house of the French Parliament, threw this out early in 1924, Poincaré was forced to resign.

In the election which followed, Poincaré's resignation, the Cartel des Gauches (Alliance of the Left) swept to power with 328 seats to the Right's 226. The Cartel was an alliance between the Radical Socialists, by now not really a left-wing party at all, and the Socialists (who had made a rapid recovery from the disaster of 1919). As the latter, although prepared to support the Radicals in Parliament, would not take up any ministerial positions, the government under Edouard Herriot was really one of the Centre Left. By the 1920s, the Radicals had become the party of the 'small man' meaning lower middle-class shopkeepers and farmers, rather than workers and peasants.

5 The Economic Crisis of 1924-6

As soon as it came into office, the Cartel des Gauches was faced with a severe economic crisis. A large part of this collapse was due to the exaggerated expectations about German reparations, the cost of reconstruction and the unwillingness of French politicians and public to contemplate higher taxation. However, there was also an element of sheer economic mismanagement. The net result of which system was that between 1921 and 1924 (when the Cartel des Gauches came to power) the expenditure of the French government had been exceeding income by between 7 and 12 billion francs per year.

The result of this chronic imbalance was the severe economic crisis of 1924 to 1926 which precipitated the collapse of the franc in these years.

The Collapse of the Franc 1924-6
Value to £ sterling

December 1924	90
December 1925	130
July 1926	240

What was the possible solution to this crisis? One was to produce an equitable taxation system which actually taxed the rich as well as the poor, but this was unacceptable to the Radicals, whose leader Edouard Herriot knew little of finance, and whose petit bourgeois supporters opposed any rise in indirect taxation. Herriot's answer was massive borrowing which only made the budget imbalance worse, and weakened the (admittedly small) amount of confidence which the business community had in a left-wing government. The word 'left' has to be used cautiously here because the Socialists who favoured heavier taxation, had, as we have seen, refused to take up any ministerial positions in the Cartel des Gauches, although they voted for Prime Minister Herriot in Parliament.

Herriot himself seemed to be more concerned about the outdated religious issue than pressing economic problems. He chose this moment to threaten the application of the 1905 Law of Separation (see page 35) to Alsace, a clear break with the position of the National Block which was designed to rally support on the Left. Instead it merely antagonised the Alsatians and did nothing to alleviate France's economic plight. In desperation, and under pressure from his Socialist allies, Herriot had to propose a 10 per cent tax on capital. When the Senate rejected this, Herriot fell from power in April 1925. He had not been prepared to recognise the realities of France's economic situation, or to introduce necessary financial reforms.

There then followed one of those dizzying periods of apparent political chaos for which the Third Republic became famous. Five cabinets came and went between April 1925 and July 1926, while the value of the franc continued to fall, and inflation increased. By the last date historians have discerned a rather desperate atmosphere in France, brought about by the collapse of the franc in a society which set great store by old-fashioned virtues like thrift and stability. Mid 1926 is seen by some as a crisis point when the whole vulnerable edifice of the post-war Republic might have collapsed. It was precisely at this point that the Republic turned again to Raymond Poincaré, the 'hard man' of French politics, for salvation.

a) Poincaré and the Government of 'National Salvation'

In July 1926 Poincaré was in a far stronger position than he had been in the early 1920s. The country's economic situation was dire and he was able to unite leading political figures (like the successful Foreign Minister Briand) in a government of so-called 'National Salvation'. Finance Minister as well as Prime Minister, Poincaré was able to bypass Parliament through the use of emergency decree laws. These provided for tax increases for all, except the very rich, whom Poincaré actually won over by reducing supertax, and the setting up of a sinking fund for France's growing national debt. Foreign loans were raised, confidence restored and the franc stabilised at one-fifth of its pre-war value. Above all, the name of Poincaré reassured the petit bourgeoisie, the small businessmen and shopkeepers who had seen their savings destroyed in the crisis between 1924 and 1926. He stood for stability, caution and private enterprise.

Why was this such a crucial period in the history of inter-war France? Primarily it seems because the lesson the business community learnt from the crisis of 1924-6 was that the Left could not be trusted with the management of France's economy while the Rightists like Poincaré could. There was a corollary to this belief, as several historians have pointed out. For the Left, embittered by its defeat in 1925, believed that the infamous Mur d'Argent (Wall of Money) composed of big business (and especially the so-called 'two hundred families' that ran the Bank of France) and industry was conspiring with the Right to keep it out of power. This belief was exaggerated, but it was a constant feature in Leftist thinking between the World Wars. The reality was that although some big financiers did have links with the Right, and especially the far Right, their political meddling was not conspicuously successful.

b) The Economic Recovery

The recovery of the French economy between 1926 and 1929 has caused at least one historian to regard it as the most remarkable economic achievement in post-war Europe. On its back, Poincaré rode to another election victory over the divided forces of the Left in 1928. He then, until ill-health forced him to retire in 1929, presided over an economic recovery which gave France an annual growth rate of 5 per cent. His stabilisation of the franc at a much lower value also meant that French goods had become very competitive in world markets. France's advance was notable in three areas. Eighty billion francs could be spent on reconstruction in the north, partly assisted by the German recovery from the hyperinflation of 1923-4 which meant that they, assisted by American loans (see page 58) could pay France more reparations. Heavy industry also boomed with coal production up and steel production doubled. Among the more modern French industries, the car industry also expanded significantly, being the world's largest manufacturer in 1929 after the USA. France really did seem to be on the road to permanent recovery and prosperity.

Poincaré could not have foreseen, of course, the worldwide economic repercussions of the Wall Street Crash of 1929. However, he is perhaps open to criticism in another area. Some historians have felt that with the economy stabilised, he should have taken the opportunity to introduce social and welfare reforms. In this sphere France, partly because of the earlier importance given to issues like religion, lagged 40 years behind Germany, and 20 years behind Britain. In fact, all that Poincaré did in this sphere was to sanction a modest programme providing insurance for the sick and aged in April 1928, with wage and salary earners contributing 5 per cent of their pay, the employers an equal amount and the State refunding the cost of an operation.

As it was, other changes to France's creaking social structure like paid holidays and an eight-hour working day were put off for another decade. Many analysts have blamed the social tensions of the 1930s on this failure to reform when times were easier. Arguably, France would have been a more effective and united society if Poincaré had seized this opportunity in 1928. Some historians have thought so, and it is possible that thoroughgoing social reform might have lessened the Left's dark suspicions of the Mur d'Argent.

6 The Issue of Stability

The economic and political events of the 1920s in France have tended to be seen to a backcloth of chronic instability and political weakness. This traditional view was presented by William Shirer and J.P.T. Bury who wrote of how France was during this period in a situation of 'veiled civil war'. It derived its evidence from the chaotic seesaw of French politics which saw governments fall in a matter of weeks, and an apparent lack of decisive political leadership. The frequent changes of government in this scenario are a key factor behind the assumption that inter-war France was virtually ungovernable, and because of this, politically, economically and militarily weak.

More recently this analysis has been challenged by several historians. Christopher Andrew, for example, has noted that the short life of French governments does not prove that the whole system was chronically unstable. On examination, the same ministers reappear in different jobs in a sort of game of political musical chairs, and because a completely left-wing government was virtually impossible in the 1920s because of the fear of Bolshevism, French governments invariably had a Centre Left or a Centre Right axis.

A right-wing government was also ruled out because, in the history of the Third Republic, the Right was associated with clericalism and reaction. This meant that right-wing parties such as the Republican

Federation and the Alliance Démocratique had to use words like 'democratic' and 'republican' in their titles if they wanted to achieve power. This also meant alliance with the centre (best represented in the 1920s by the Radicals) which was constantly in government. This provided a continuity of personnel in government which caused a contemporary French observer to coin the phrase 'a Republic of pals' to describe the Third Republic of his day. One example serves to underline this point. Edouard Daladier, a leading figure in the Radical party throughout the inter-war period, served in every French cabinet between 1926 and 1940.

Another historian, J.F. MacMillan, has challenged the old stereotype of the Third Republic from another angle. First of all he cautions against acceptance of the idea that France was rent by ideological divisions between Right and Left. Rather, he argues, was it a case of consensus in the centre of French politics which ran the country and shunned extremes. Ideological arguments in his view made a lot of noise but were not ultimately that important. Going further still, MacMillan suggests that the fragmentation of political opinion in France in many parties, far from being a weakness was a sign of political life and vibrancy (by contrast with the rather stolid British and their three-party system). This system was one that suited the French and despite appearances to the contrary, worked. Only if the criterion used was the longevity of governments could France be seen as unstable and ungovernable, and then only because too much notice was being taken of noisy Left-Right debates. Both wings were effectively excluded from real power.

This challenging thesis has been valuable because it makes historians (and students) look beyond the shifting sands of French politics at what was really happening under the surface in French society. Its vulnerability may lie in perhaps discounting the effects which constant changes of government had in the key sectors of foreign policy-making and management of the economy. The evidence does also seem to suggest that suspicion of the Left was a real factor in causing a rush to invest abroad, during its brief periods of real power. Nonetheless, MacMillan presents a trenchant case for the viability and resourcefulness of the Third Republic between 1918 and 1940. 'Democracy in France then was not a mere sham, nor was it in a state of "decadence", reflecting a chronic incapacity for government on the part of the French.'

7 The Depression and its Economic Consequences

The collapse of the United States' economy in 1929 had profound worldwide effects. As far as France was concerned, they were twofold. First, the cancellation of American loans to Germany meant that the Germans could not continue the reparations payments on which France placed so much reliance. Second, the effect of the French devaluation of

1926 which had made exports more competitive was neutralised. The luxury goods in which France specialised were especially badly hit and the country became a dumping ground for cheaper foreign manufactured goods which were exported because the domestic markets had collapsed.

The overall effects of the Depression were dramatic. French exports were down by 40 per cent between 1929 and 1932. Production fell drastically at home so, for example, steel output fell by 40 per cent between 1930 and 1935. At the same time France which had virtually full employment in the 1920s had over 400,000 unemployed by 1935, and many others were on half-time working.

Severe recession demanded drastic measures, but they were not forthcoming. One response of government, tried equally ineffectively elsewhere, was tariff protection. Increased duties on foreign goods did not though counteract the fall in world prices since 1929. As French governments continued to be unwilling to raise taxation, state revenues fell, and very little was done to help the unemployed and those sectors of French society which were badly hit by the Depression.

When in 1932 a Radical government was returned under Herriot (with Socialist support) it offered a deflationary package based on cuts in expenditure and finally grasping the nettle, an increase in taxes. This outraged the Right but also failed to get Socialist support as Blum's party feared being associated with such an unpopular measure. At the same time public opinion was infuriated by a demand from the USA for repayment of part of France's war debt. When Herriot, having failed to pass his budget, tried to get the debt repayment through Parliament he was defeated and forced to resign.

Thereafter successive cabinets lasted forty days, nine months and three weeks. Ultimately another radical administration under Chautemps managed to pass virtually the same budget proposals that had helped to bring down the Herriot government in 1932. This time the Socialists, to quote one historian, 'cravenly absented themselves' from Parliament so they could avoid association with an unpopular budget, but also the accusation that they had brought down yet another cabinet.

The debate about France's political stability is particularly pertinent in any analysis of her economic management. True, if the Andrew thesis is accepted, the constant changes of government may not have been a sign of political weakness, but the executive weakness apparent to foreign investors can surely have done little to strengthen France's economic position. Chronic unwillingness from 1918 onwards to take unpopular economic decisions put the franc under severe pressure and deprived governments of the necessary leverage to counter crises like those that occurred in 1924 and 1929. When tough decisions were made, as in 1926, France's economy showed its traditional resilience. Yet these decisions were made, it must be noted, when Poincaré had been granted extra-parliamentary powers which allowed him to circumvent parliamentary opposition. Christopher Andrew has also been forced to admit that there was something of a 'culture of opposition' in France whereby deputies were unduly obstructive and did not always consider the national interest. Nowhere arguably was this tendency to oppose strong measures on principle, more destructive than in the economic sector which demanded both continuity in policy and stability in society.

8 The Political Crisis

Reference has already been made to a possible opportunity for basic reform which was missed by Poincaré in 1928, but a plan for thoroughgoing economic and social reform which might have alleviated its consequences initially, came not from the Left, but from the right-winger André Tardieu. He was Prime Minister for most of the period 1929 to 1932 (with a short gap in 1930), and when historians have said that the great figures of the Republic (like Clemenceau and Poincaré) had gone by the 1930s, they have tended to forget Tardieu. He it was who proposed a five-year plan to modernise agriculture and industry, and to introduce public works schemes for building houses, schools and hospitals (precisely the methods used to combat the Depression in the USA), but Tardieu was widely distrusted by both the Centre and the Left, and his scheme was rejected. Was an even bigger opportunity for an overhaul of the French system missed in 1930? Certainly, none of Tardieu's political opponents had anything better to offer.

Tardieu was a strong anti-Communist, and fear of communism was a characteristic of the growth of the extreme Right in the years of the Depression, for France, like Germany and Italy, had its fascist movements and in the 1930s, and they seemed to be a significant political menace to the parliamentary system. Historians have pondered about exactly what it was about French society which avoided the slide into authoritarian, or even totalitarian, rule.

Part of the answer seems to lie with the personalities of the leaders of the leagues (the usual name for the fascist movements). One of the most influential was Charles Maurras, the leader of the Action Française, but he was essentially an intellectual and not a man of action. Supposedly a Catholic and a monarchist, Maurras was regarded with suspicion by the Church (Pope Pius XI denounced Action Française in 1926) because of his self-obsession and disinterest in the welfare of the masses. This was shown by his reactionary opposition to mass primary education.

Although his movement was anti-Communist and anti-Semitic, both characteristics of fascist parties, Maurras cannot really be described as a fascist. He was too aloof to be a French Hitler.

The other main movement of the extreme Right was 'the Cross of Fire' *(Croix de Feu)* led by Colonel de la Rocque, whose exact beliefs were obscure. The Cross of Fire, though anti-Communist, was not anti-Semitic and de la Rocque condemned violence. Its greatest appeal lay with the ex-servicemen's organisations in which pacifism was a strong influence. However, there were genuine fascist groups in France such as the Blueshirts, Cagoulards (Hooded Men) and Greenshirts, the latter being peasant fascists who wanted to go back to a more rural life-style, but if the membership of all these groups was only 150,000 in the early 1930s, why were they regarded as being so significant? The answer to this question links the leagues with the major political scandal of 1934 which seemed to endanger the life of the Republic itself.

a) The Stavisky Affair

Sacha Stavisky (alias Serge Alexandre) was arrested in January 1934 by the police in Chamonix, but in circumstances which were never satisfactorily explained he was then able to commit suicide. Stavisky was wanted for floating a fraudulent loan worth millions of francs supposedly to finance the municipal pawnshop of Bayonne. However, a trial of fraud and wrongdoing led all the way back to 1926, with numerous arrests of Stavisky and mysterious releases resulting from his links with leading figures in French society. One of these, the public prosecutor in Paris, who had ordered the fraudster's release on several occasions, happened to be the brother-in-law of the Radical party premier Camille Chautemps. Few French people believed the suicide story. Many thought that Stavisky was killed because of his embarrassing links with government circles. Such suspicions were strengthened when Prime Minister Chautemps refused to order an enquiry into Stavisky's death.

Here was the great cause which the far Right could use as a means of attacking the parliamentary democracy which they so much hated. No sooner had the news of Stavisky's death become known in Paris than rightist mobs were out on the streets chanting 'Down with the Robbers, Down with the Assassins!' Spasmodic anti-government rioting continued with the end of January 1934, reaching a crescendo on 27 January when mobs threatened the parliament building and frightened Chautemps into resignation.

b) The Crisis of 6 February 1934

Chautemps was succeeded as premier by Edouard Daladier, another Radical, who immediately promised to set up a parliamentary committee to investigate the Stavisky affair. He also enraged the leagues by sacking the then Paris police chief who was hated by the Socialists because of his extreme right-wing sympathies.

During the evening of 6 February, therefore, the leagues poured on to the streets of Paris and prepared to attack the Chamber of Deputies building where the Deputies were debating the situation while the mob howled for blood outside. One of the most extraordinary aspects of the situation was that the Communists, acting on instructions from Stalin in Moscow, joined in with the Fascists of the Cross of Fire in their attack on the Republican regime. This was because the Soviet dictator had produced a bizarre theory that assisting a fascist takeover of power would eventually assist a Communist victory because fascism was the highest and last stage of capitalism. According to the theory, the defenders of the Republic (the Socialists and Radicals) were 'social fascists' who were the enemies of the working class in France.

Confused fighting outside the parliament building between rioters and the police resulted in 14 deaths and hundreds of casualties. Well-known Deputies like Herriot only narrowly avoided being thrown into the River Seine, but the police lines held and the parliament building was not assaulted. Nevertheless, Daladier, like Chautemps before him, felt obliged to resign following the events of February 6. Two prime ministers of France, therefore, had been forced out of office by the threat of violence, a unique development in the history of the Third Republic.

c) 6 February 1934: A Revolutionary Situation?

In the half century since 1934 there has been a good deal of controversy about the importance of what happened on 6 February. At the time, the view taken depended on the political affiliation of the person or persons concerned. Thus the fascist R. Brasillach described what happened as 'an instinctive and magnificent revolt'.

The Left reacted quite differently, and within days the Communists changed their perspective in line with new orders from Moscow which at last recognised the fascist threat not just in France but throughout Europe. Communists and Socialists alike saw what happened as part of a deliberate conspiracy by the far Right to overthrow the Republic (the former's shabby role in what happened in February 1934 being conveniently forgotten). This was the orthodox view of the French Left for many years, one that was endorsed by the post-war 1946 parliamentary commission of enquiry which concluded that:

> the Sixth of February was a revolt against Parliament, an attack against the regime. The intention was, by means of a popular uprising, to disperse the deputies, to take possession of the Chamber and to proclaim an authoritarian government.

Modern historians have been unable to accept this view, having failed to find conclusive evidence for the existence of a common plan or conspiracy between the various fascist groupings (the PCF was acting on its own initiative) to bring down the Third Republic. They tend instead to see what happened on 6 February 1934 as a spasm of frustrated rage by the far Right against the parliamentary regime which they so hated, and had no chance of really influencing through the ballot box. Only in the hour of France's defeat in 1940 and occupation by the Germans were the French Fascists to have their day.

The true importance of what happened on 6 February seems to lie in its impact on the French Left. Even if the Left's analysis of the events is now thought to be faulty, there is no doubt about its unifying effect on the Communists, Socialists and Radicals.

In 1935 a Popular Front which united the parties of the Left was formed in France which was to win the general election of 1936. This was a response to the perceived threat from the far Right, and meant that in France at least fascism was faced by a united Left. The irony is that this unity was achieved as a result of an uprising which almost certainly lacked the capacity to overthrow the Republic.

9 The Rise of the Popular Front

The essential point about the common programme which united the Communists, Socialists and Radicals in the Front Populaire (Popular Front) in 1935, was that it was moderate enough not to alienate the Radicals. Its basic features were to be a ban on the fascist leagues in France, and the destruction of the influence of the so-called 'Two Hundred Families'. The Communists bent over backwards to get Radical agreement and even put out friendly feelers to the Catholic Church (predictably they were not accepted).

Other events in 1935 were a reminder of the viciousness of the far Right. First, Charles Maurras denounced the Socialist leader Léon Blum as 'a monster of the republic' and 'a man to be shot but only in the back', and then Blum himself was attacked by a mob when he had the misfortune to drive into an Action Française funeral procession for one of its leaders. Crying 'Death to the Jew' the mob pulled Blum out of his car and kicked and beat him as he lay in the road. Only the prompt intervention of workers from a nearby building site saved Blum from possible death.

Maurras subsequently served four months in jail for incitement to murder, but Blum's injuries were severe enough to prevent him campaigning in the general election called for April 1936. The attack on him served, however, to bring the Left closer together as a huge pro-Blum demonstration in Paris showed a few days later, and in the election itself, the Left swept to victory with the Communists picking up 62 extra seats, and the Socialists a further 39. National interest in the campaign was reflected in the huge turnout with the result that 'the left had won its most famous victory'.

French Communists demonstrate in the streets of Paris on 9 February 1934

a) The Popular Front in Power

After the Popular Front victory at the polls, Léon Blum assumed the position of Prime Minister because he was the leader of the largest party. However, because the Socialists did not have an outright majority in Parliament Blum did not believe that he had a mandate for radical reform and this was to have important consequences. His position was further weakened by the fact that the Communists decided to stay out of the Popular Front government, claiming that their membership of it would provoke panic. This was really an excuse for non-involvement in the decision-making process, which allowed the PCF to snipe at the government from the sidelines when unpopular decisions had to be made. For their part, the Radicals formed a coalition government with the Socialists only on the condition that there would be no devaluation of the franc and no exchange controls (which might have prevented conservative investors sending their money abroad). From the outset, therefore, the Popular Front government seemed to be hedged about with obstacles.

By contrast the working class was in a mood of expectancy, even of euphoria, that at last its government was in power. Oddly perhaps the victory of the Popular Front was followed by a great wave of strikes and occupation of factories throughout France as Blum prepared to take office. This was partly a protest against poor wages and conditions, but also a reminder to the government that it should not renege on the promises in the common programme. A million workers were involved.

The man who was expected to fulfil the workers' expectations was Léon Blum. He was a Jewish lawyer who had worked as a government adviser and a lawyer before becoming a Socialist deputy. Blum had always been an anti-Marxist who wished to strengthen the institutions of the Third Republic by protecting individual liberties, but he had long wrestled with the issue of whether Socialists should enter government with bourgeois parties. Only the conviction that there was a genuine fascist threat in France convinced Blum of the need to accept the premiership in 1936. As outlined above he knew from personal experience what the hatred of the far Right could mean, and it coined a new and sinister slogan 'Better Hitler than Blum'.

Blum had promised the Radicals that he would not devalue the franc again, but otherwise he honoured his pledges by means of the Matignon Agreement, signed by unions, employers and the State in June 1936. A great raft of reforms was brought in:

Article One   the employers agree to the establishment of collective agreements.

Article Two   these agreements, in particular, must embody Articles Three and Five below.

Article Three within the requirements of all citizens to obey the law, the employers recognise the freedom of opinion of the workers and their right freely to join and to belong to trade unions established in conformity with the Labour Code...

Article Four with effect from 25 May 1936, and upon the resumption of work, the wages of all workers will be raised by a scale ranging from 15 per cent for the lowest paid to 7 per cent for the highest paid. In no case will the total increase in any establishment be greater than 12 per cent. Increases already conceded since 25 May 1936 will be counted towards these increases. But higher increases already awarded will continue to operate. The negotiations for the collective settlement of minimum wages by regions and by occupations, which the parties agreed to initiate at once, must in particular, take up essential revision of abnormally low wage rates.

Article Five with the exception of special cases already determined by law, each establishment containing more than ten workers shall ... have at least two shop stewards.

Article Six the employers promise no reprisals will be taken against workers.

Once the agreement had been signed, the CGT agreed that all its workers should go back to work. Further articles provided for a 40-hour working week and two weeks' paid holiday a year, both innovations in France.

Blum's government also introduced a further measure to nationalise arms manufacturers, 'the merchants of death' who were hated by the Left, and closer State supervision of the Bank of France. This was to counteract the influence of the 'Two Hundred Families'. Another significant change was the establishment of the 'Office of Wheat' to stabilise the price of wheat, and address the problems which had been caused by falling prices in the countryside. Direct government intervention in this way was an innovation.

The effect of all these reforms was briefly to re-establish the faith of the industrial proletariat in the State, but the euphoria of April-June 1936 did not last. Initially it was foreign policy which caused the trouble because of disagreements with the Communists about supporting the Spanish Republic (see page 59), but the major problems facing the Popular Front were, as was generally the case in the inter-war period, economic.

The immediate response from the employers to the State enforced Matignon Agreement was hostility. As a class, they had been profoundly shocked by the industrial militancy of the summer of 1936, and the implied threat to the authority of *le patron* (the boss). More seriously for the Popular Front the economic consequences of Blum's reforms proved to be largely negative. Production, despite the carrot of paid holidays and the 40-hour week did not rise and was still down even on the levels of 1929. Prices also continued to rise so that Blum, despite his pre-election pledge to the Radicals, was forced to devalue the franc in the autumn of 1936. Even then the devaluation did not go far enough, and French goods still remained uncompetitive in world markets.

Exchange controls which might have stabilised the value of the franc were not considered by Blum, he said, because 'they will have the fatal effect of straining the ties which unite us to the Anglo-Saxon democracies, ties which are essential to the coherent development of our foreign policy'. In the late 1930s France was to be consistently dependent on US and British financial help, which meant that Blum could never contemplate introducing a truly socialist programme involving wholesale nationalisation (neither did he have the needed support in Parliament). Neither as we have seen did he believe that he had an electoral mandate for such change.

The net result of this economic weakness was that in March 1937 Blum was forced to announce a 'pause' in the government's reform programme and a general impression of impotence prevailed. Even in the area where executive action should have been effective in banning the fascist leagues it was not, for they merely reappeared disguised as political parties like the French Social Party.

Ultimately, as it had always threatened to do, economic and financial policy brought the Popular Front down in June 1937. Blum demanded special emergency powers to allow the government to repay its debts but the Senate refused. As the Radicals had already refused to back even the most modest tax increases, Blum had little option but to resign. The Popular Front experiment had lasted barely a year.

b) The Failure and Significance of the Popular Front

The supporters of the Popular Front were to claim that it was destroyed by its capitalist enemies. The 'Wall of Money' according to this theory was responsible for a 'flight of capital' out of France in 1936-7 which forced Blum to abandon his reform programme, and ultimately brought down his government. It was certainly true that industry and commerce had no faith in the economic policies of the Front, and believed that its social reforms as set out in the Matignon Agreement were too expensive. This does not prove, however, that the Right alone was responsible for sabotaging Blum's government.

Another significant factor in the failure of the Popular Front was the lack of unity on the Left itself, a consistent feature of French inter-war politics. The economic conservatism of the Radicals, Blum's doubts about his popular mandate and the rightness of co-operation with the Radicals, all combined with the negative attitude of the Communists to make the achievement of a really radical reform programme almost impossible. Historians have noted that the Matignon Agreement was essentially a compromise between industry and commerce and a government which was as worried as the employers that the workers were getting out of hand.

Yet they have continued to regard the period of the first Popular Front government as a significant watershed in modern French history. For some, the social reforms of the Front in themselves mark a significant turning point. Others contrast the working-class radicalism of 1936 with other great periods of working-class militancy in France like 1848 and 1871, and emphasise how the French Left at least did recognise the seriousness of the fascist threat in Europe.

More right-wing historians put forward another case. This accuses the Front of weakening French industry with its expensive reforms at a time when the country needed to rearm quickly in the face of an aggressive Nazi Germany. Economic mismanagement by the Front (and it is certainly true that the devaluation of the franc was delayed too long) is also blamed for both the flight of capital out of France in 1936-7 and the unwillingness of foreigners to invest in her economy. This economic weakness is often linked to France's catastrophic military defeat in the summer of 1940.

Are such accusations fair? It seems wrong to blame the Popular Front for France's later defeat when it spent at least as much money on rearmament as other governments, and was probably more aware of the threat posed by Nazism. However, the reforms of 1936-7 were undoubtedly very expensive, even if long overdue, and may have contributed to the financial crisis which eventually brought down the Blum government. Having said this, the legend of the 'Mur d'Argent' though clearly exaggerated does have some relevance to the fate of the Popular Front. This was because any government of the Left in France in the mid-1930s would have been a victim of capitalist suspicion. The situation was made worse for the Popular Front both by the level of social spending needed to try to appease its own supporters, and the increasingly dangerous international situation which demanded more spending on armaments (it is true that the nationalisation of armaments firms only caused confusion in the short run). Unity amongst its own supporters might have allowed the Blum government to survive longer, but would hardly have resolved the policy dilemmas facing it.

Nowhere perhaps was the policy dilemma facing the Popular Front sharper than in foreign affairs, and this had severe consequences for its unity. Everything in Blum's background would make him sympathetic to the Spanish Republic in its struggle with the rebel Franco and his fascist allies Germany and Italy. He was under severe pressure from the French Communists to aid the Republic and in the initial stages of the Spanish Civil War he did so. Yet ultimately a complex inter-meshing of domestic and foreign policy factors caused him to opt for non-intervention.

On the one hand Blum feared that heavy involvement in Spain would provoke the Right and cause civil war in France itself, and on the other, he knew that his major ally Britain was strongly opposed to intervention on the side of the Republic. It was a situation in which Blum could not win because the policy of non-intervention alienated the Communists who withdrew their support from the Front. Given, therefore, the complexity of the problems facing the Popular Front it is not surprising that many historians have concluded that its failure was inevitable.

There was a melancholy sequel to the experience of the first Popular Front government. In 1938 Blum was briefly Prime Minister again after successive Radical administrations had failed to grapple with the economic legacy left by the Popular Front. This time Blum tried to persuade the Right to join the Popular Front in a government of national unity (similar to that headed by Poincaré in 1926), but the Right hated him too much for this to be feasible, and the government lasted barely a month. By the end of the year 1938, the Popular Front itself had been dissolved.

10 The Daladier Government

For its last two years of life, the Third Republic looked to Edouard Daladier as its saviour. A former history professor, the 'bull of Vaucluse' had his admirers, and certainly did not lack governmental experience. Already Prime Minister three times by 1938, Daladier had been in no less than 25 Cabinets. He was also on the more radical wing of his party and had persuaded colleagues to join the Popular Front in 1935.

Yet, the figure which looks out from contemporary newsreels often seems tormented and careworn, while puffing away at the obligatory Gauloise cigarette. He was said to drink too much, but he retained genuine popularity among the people. Unlike Blum he was not a divisive figure, although his period in office marked a much tougher and less-accommodating attitude to the workers. Like his party, Daladier moved sharply to the right in 1938, breaking all links with the Popular Front, and won some support from former right-wing voters.

The Right-Centre axis of the new government was immediately evident in efforts to dismantle the reforms of the Popular Front. Derogation or exemptions from the rule about a 40-hour week were given to firms on the orders of Daladier and his new Finance Minister, Paul Reynaud. On a personal level the two men had little time for one another (this antipathy extended to their mistresses), but on one thing they did agree, the need to get rid of the 40-hour week. Without such a reform Daladier believed it would be impossible to revive production and pay for the fourfold increase in armaments spending which Reynaud announced late in 1938.

In line with a new and more rigorous financial policy, public expenditure was also cut, and the price controls instituted by the

Popular Front scrapped. One of the earliest moves of the Daladier government had been to devalue the franc again by 10 per cent in May 1938, despite some murmurings within his own Radical party. However, all these moves were assisted by Daladier's alliance with the Right which created a feeling of security in financial circles so that investment money began to flow back into France. He was also assisted by the decision of the Senate to give him the financial powers which it had refused to Blum. The net result of the Daladier/Reynaud economic strategy was that after years of decline France began to develop a more vigorous economy.

There was a price to pay for this economic revival and it was paid, unsurprisingly, by organised labour. The trade unions were incensed by the attempts to renege on the 40-hour week, and they had already been provoked by bosses who had been dragging their feet on the Matignon Agreement and sacking shop stewards. The classic response to such provocation was the general strike, and the Communist CGTU called one for the end of November 1938. This time, however, the circumstances were quite unlike 1936 and the general strike was a fiasco. The government was prepared to take tough action against the strikers by mobilising troops and police, and strikers were driven out of the Renault car works by tear gas. Strikers were also sacked, or even prosecuted, and the general strike received a poor response. Only 2 per cent of railwaymen, for example, came out on strike.

The relationship between economics and politics was very close here because Daladier linked his attack on the CGTU with another on the PCF itself. Communist newspapers were shut down and Communist deputies in the Chamber harassed by the police. All this was because Daladier, faced with a growing threat from Nazi Germany, could claim a new authority with the French people. He was an old style patriot, telling French people that, '...I am the son of a worker, and I am a patriot...,' and he evoked similar feelings in the people be they left- or right-wing in their political leanings.

11 Decadence or Recovery?

The most vigorous historical debate about the history of inter-war France has been about the question of whether she was in sharp decline in the years down to 1940, or whether, as historians have more recently suggested, there was a meaningful and vigorous revival between the Munich Conference of September 1938 and the outbreak of the Second World War in September 1939. Part of this argument properly belongs to the domain of foreign affairs (see page 74), but important sections of it relate to the economy and the contemporary perception which the French people had of themselves.

Important work has been done since the 1970s by Professor Duroselle to the effect that public opinion polls taken in 1938-9 contradict the old stereotype of French defeatism, and economic and political decline. Instead the polls showed a more optimistic mood at home, and a tougher attitude towards aggressor powers such as Germany and Italy abroad. Duroselle has also made the link between the quickening of French industrial production in 1938-9 and the remarkable progress made in the sphere of aerial rearmament (citing the work of notable French economic historians).

An American historian, Robert Young, has also pointed out that the French educational system taught children to be proud of the empire and the country's cultural tradition, while other research has supported the view that in 1938-9 Daladier was a genuinely popular leader who brought about a real psychological change in France in the 12 months before war broke out in 1939.

There is still a 'decadence school' amongst modern historians, however. The Frenchman René Girault has identified a chronic lack of political will in addressing France's problems which, he argues, was brought about by a genuine division in French society between those who feared communism and those who loathed the fascists. This division brought about political paralysis.

Girault recognises the extent of French economic recovery in 1938-9, but says that it came too late. The economy had already been fatally weakened by the 'flight of capital' under the Popular Front and the costly reforms introduced by Blum's government. Curiously also Duroselle belongs to the decadence school. Disallowing his own research on the French recovery, he still highlights the role of reactionary defeatists like Marshal Pétain (Defence Minister in several governments), and the fatal weaknesses in the constitution which gave France a weak executive and a too powerful Parliament. Between 1932 and 1940 alone this resulted in 16 changes of government, and a fatal lack of strong leadership so that when war came 'men proved weaker than fate'.

This debate is extremely important, for if France was a divided and enfeebled society in 1939, then her defeat in the Second World War can be linked directly to economic and constitutional factors. If she did in fact begin a vigorous recovery in 1938-9 then military factors loom up as the primary causes of the disaster in May-June 1940. There is still much debate on the military side (see page 85).

12 Conclusion

It is, in the end, a remarkable fact that despite its persistent economic crises, the excesses of the far Right and the militancy of the Communists, the Third Republic did survive when other democratic regimes in Germany, Italy and Spain did not. The end came in the wake of military defeat in 1940, not as a result of internal revolution.

This shows that France did have a solid democratic core. It was personified, for all their flaws by men like Poincaré, Blum and Daladier.

Politics   **Economics**

Fall of Clemenceau

Left excluded from power

Fascist threat?

Political and social reforms of the Popular Front

The reparations issue

Weak franc and devaluation

Depression and effects

Recovery and rearmament

Summary - 'Reconstruction and Economic Crisis 1918-39'

Making notes on *'Reconstruction and Economic Crisis 1918-39'*

This chapter has dealt with the various crises facing inter-war French governments. The following note headings should help you to highlight the most important aspects.
1   Post-war Reconstruction.
1.1 The price of victory.
1.2 The reparations question.
1.3 The fall of Clemenceau.
2   The Economic Crisis in the 1920s.
2.1 The socialist-communist split.
2.2 The economic crisis 1924-6.
2.3 Poincaré and economic recovery.
3   The Economic and Political Results of the Depression.
3.1 The economic crisis after 1930.
3.2 The Stavisky affair. Causes and consequences.
3.3 The uprising of 6 February 1934 and its significance.
3.4 The formation of the Popular Front.
4   The Popular Front.
4.1 Working-class expectations.
4.2 The Popular Front reforms.
4.3 The economic problems of the Popular Front and its fall.
5   Daladier and recovery.
5.1 Abandonment of Popular Front reforms.
5.2 The repression of organised labour.
5.3 Evidence for a French recovery. The debate.

Answering essay questions on *'Reconstruction and Economic Crisis'*

Questions are likely to focus on distinctive political and economic issues.

It may be helpful for prospective titles to be grouped under these separate headings.

Political

1   Account for the fall of Clemenceau so soon after he had led France to victory in 1918.
2   Assess the importance of the split in the France Left in 1920.
3   Were the demonstrations of 6 February 1934 'a revolt against Parliament'?
4   Account for the rise and fall of the Popular Front.

Economic

5   Why did reparations fail to solve France's economic problems in the 1920s?
6   How significant an influence was the Depression on French history in the 1930s?

Even if the primary focus of the essay title is political or economic, there will always be a degree of overlap. In Question 4, for example, you will need to be aware of the economic causes of the collapse of the Popular Front, even if the creation of the Front was a result of the apparent threat from the far Right. Certain key words in A Level questions appear again, like 'assess' and 'significant'. They demand that you make a judgement on a particular issue as in Questions 2 and 6. At the core of Question 6, for example, must be a judgement on the importance of the Depression rather than just a recitation of facts about what it meant.

Source-based questions on 'Reconstruction and Economic Crisis 1918-39'

The Costs of Victory, and the Matignon Agreement
Study the statistical tables on pages 30 and 37, and Article 4 of the extract on pages 47 and 48. Answer the following questions.

a)   Using the information on page 30 explain the statement 'The glory of 1918 was therefore purchased at a hideous price'. (2 marks)
b)   What links can you find between the two sets of statistics on pages 30 and 37? (5 marks)
c)   Explain how the concessions made in Article 4 of the extract on pages 47 and 48 could contribute to a situation similar to that suggested by the figures on page 37. (5 marks)
d)   What principle do you think Article 4 of the extract is trying to enforce? Use the material in the extract to support your argument. (5 marks)
e)   Use all the sources to outline the nature of the problems facing the Third Republic between 1918 and 1939. (8 marks)

CHAPTER 4

The Search for Security 1919-39

In 1919 France had two major foreign policy preoccupations: to make Germany pay for the damage she had done in the war (the issue of reparations had considerable domestic ramifications) and to safeguard her own security for the future.

1 Versailles: An Excuse for Vengeance?

The instrument for attaining these objectives was to be, in French eyes, the Treaty of Versailles drawn up in Louis XIV's old palace near to Paris, and signed by all the great powers, except Russia, on 28 June 1919. In that same palace France herself had been forced to accept humiliating defeat at the hands of a newly-united Germany in 1871.

The Treaty contained detailed reparations clauses and the French position on reparations has been outlined on pages 31-2. Otherwise the French were concerned with crippling Germany's military power, and this intention can be seen in those clauses of the Treaty which reduced the German army to 100,000 men, created a demilitarised zone on the left bank of the River Rhine, and gave France access to the coalmines of the Saar. Possession of the Saar mines also enshrined the principle of compensation for damage done by the German army in France. Natural justice also seemed to be served by the return to France of Alsace-Lorraine, annexed by Germany in 1871.

Even then, many Frenchmen were not satisfied with the settlement and believed that Germany should have been partitioned, as she was to be after her defeat in 1945. Foch, among others, encouraged so-called 'separatism' in Germany whereby individual states like Bavaria might secede from the German state. So in this context Georges Clemenceau, often regarded as an intransigent nationalist determined to exact every ounce of money or territory from Germany, might seem quite moderate. One thing was certain in 1919, all Frenchmen were united in their recognition that German militarism must be curbed. But France did not, as we have seen, initially press for punitive reparations against Germany.

This is a very important point to remember in the debate about the alleged severity of the Versailles Treaty, much of it provoked by the book called *The Economic Consequences of the Peace* written in 1919 by the celebrated British economist, John Maynard Keynes. A stereotype was created of France as a vengeful, aggrieved power anxious to cripple Germany permanently and to alter the balance of power in Europe in its favour. Yet even had France wished to do this, she could not have done so, first because her British and American allies would not allow it, and second because it was not possible. Germany's military and industrial potential was so great that recovery was inevitable whatever restrictions the Treaty of Versailles placed upon her. Clemenceau fully recognised Germany's daunting power, despite her defeat in the First World War, when he warned his fellow countrymen and women, 'Mark well what I'm telling you. In six months, in a year, in five years, ten years, or as they like, the Boches will again invade us'.

This created the central dilemma of French foreign policy in the inter-war period. Harsh treatment of Germany might embitter her (the Treaty of Versailles did that anyway), but what was the alternative? Especially when in 1919 Clémentel's generous initiative about reparations (see page 31) was rejected by France's allies. Modern historians have recognised the extent of France's dilemma when confronting a neighbour with almost double its population and vastly greater resources. A contemporary Frenchman described the Treaty of Versailles as being *'trop douce pour ce qu'elle a de dur'* (too mild for its severity) and Sally Marks has endorsed this view. Writing of the Treaty she remarks that it was 'too soft to restrain Germany and yet too severe to be acceptable to most Germans'. The Treaty should either have been 'more French', that is more punitive, or 'more Wilsonian' (a reference to the more sympathetic views of the USA's President Wilson) by seeking to reconcile Germany with the Allies by lenient treatment.

Crucially, a second historian, Antony Lentin, has pointed out, 'the peace of restitution and security that would compensate France for her inherent and increased disparity and free her from fear of attack' was not forthcoming. Lentin rejects the idea put forward by Keynes and the Germans that Versailles was 'a slave treaty'. Neither does he accept Mark's belief in a possible Wilsonian solution. Instead, he argues, its very lack of severity created the nightmare that France so feared, the likelihood of a recovered, vengeful Germany demanding wholesale revision of the Versailles settlement. This perhaps begs the question of whether any treaty, however severe, could have succeeded in curbing German power after 1919.

Yet there was a realistic alternative to trying to grind Germany down. The League of Nations was created in 1919 and its founding charter was incorporated into the Versailles Treaty. This stated that one of its aims was to preserve the international peace through the principle of 'collective security'. All member states would in theory unite against a potential aggressor.

The League Covenant was based on President Woodrow Wilson's famous Fourteen Points of 1918, his reaction to the German request for peace terms. Clemenceau's response to the concept of the League was sceptical. He remarked memorably that France had no need of Fourteen Points as 'the Lord God had only ten!' but he was prepared to accept Wilson's proposal for a League of Nations providing that French security was safeguarded by a tripartite military alliance between France, Britain and the United States. With such security France would not, arguably, need to coerce Germany. Sadly for France, and for

Europe too, the Anglo-American guarantee of a military alliance given in 1919 was reneged upon. The United States, despite Wilson's promptings, refused to join the League, to honour the guarantee, or even to sign the Versailles Treaty. Britain then used American refusal as an excuse to refuse to sign a military agreement with France. Subsequent French policy had to be formulated, therefore, in the knowledge that Clemenceau had tried, and failed, to obtain real security for his country in 1919.

2 The Policy of Coercion

One French response to German claims that they could not pay reparations was coercion, a policy associated with Raymond Poincaré. As early as 1920 German attempts to evade reparations payments had been followed by French occupation of the towns of Frankfurt and Darmstadt, but this punitive French policy did not meet British approval.

a) The Ruhr Invasion

Anglo-French relations reached their nadir in 1923 when Poincaré used a German reparations default (actually over a consignment of telegraph poles) to send French troops into the Ruhr, Germany's largest industrial area. Belgium supported French action by sending in troops as well, but Britain flatly refused to do so.

Poincaré's action backfired badly. German workers began a campaign of passive resistance, and edgy French soldiers shot some of them dead in the big Krupp steelworks in Essen. The French also deported all the German police and other officials from the Ruhr, and tried to work the coalmines and steelmills themselves. None of these tactics worked. Instead the French had to agree to the calling of an international conference in London in 1924, where the British and Americans joined them in discussion about the reparations issue. The result of these talks was the Dawes Plan which both scaled down Germany's reparations payments and gave her longer to pay. All French troops were to withdraw from the Ruhr.

In support of French policy it can be argued that the Ruhr intervention did result in a review of the reparations machinery, which meant that France received regular payments over the next five years. Was the price worth paying? Historians have not generally thought so, first because German opinion was outraged (especially by France's use of black colonial troops) and second because the Ruhr intervention effectively closed down Germany's main industrial area. This in turn contributed to the hyperinflation of the mark in Germany in 1923-4 when the currency became virtually worthless.

Most damaging of all was the effect of French action in 1923 on relations with Britain and the USA (although isolationist in foreign policy, the Americans still wanted their money back). Both powers were infuriated by French behaviour and retaliated by putting pressure on the franc. Between January 1923, when French troops went into the Ruhr, and March 1924 the value of the franc against the US dollar went down from 15 to 26 with catastrophic effects on the domestic economy (see page 37). The fact that France also owed Britain and the USA $30 billion in war loans meant that Poincaré, seeing the failure of his attempt to coerce Germany, had little option but to agree to the Dawes Plan.

b) The Eastern Pacts

If Germany could not be coerced into paying her reparations, she might be coerced into good behaviour by a series of alliances between France and other states. This was the other major feature of French foreign policy in the early 1920s. 'Collective Security' was the key phrase of the day, but for French governments it meant only one thing - the neutralisation of the German threat.

The focus of French attention was Central and Eastern Europe, but they had one major problem. Unlike in the years before 1914 when France had relied on Russia as her major ally, this option was no longer available. Alliance with Bolshevik Russia was unacceptable to centre-right or centre-left French governments until the 1930s because of their fear of, and hostility to, communism. So the alternative was a series of alliances with the small, new states of Central and Eastern Europe - Poland in 1921, Czechoslovakia in 1924, Romania in 1926 and Yugoslavia in 1927.

It was not, however, a very satisfactory alternative for only the Franco-Polish Treaty of 1921 resembled the old Franco-Russian Treaty of 1894 in having a clear commitment from each power to help its ally if it was attacked by Germany. The other agreements merely referred to the principle, enshrined in the League of Nations Covenant, of states mutually guaranteeing each other's territory. No-one was sure what this might mean in wartime. Neither were any talks held between the French, Czech, Romanian or Yugoslav military to decide their response in the event of war breaking out.

A fog of uncertainty, therefore, surrounded France's relationship with her Eastern European allies. Would she aid them in the event of war? More importantly, would they prove to be an adequate replacement for the old Russian alliance? Might not the ethnic hatreds of the area (most Poles, for example, detested Czechs) drag France into localised squabbles? Some Frenchmen noted that, ominously, the Germans called the small Eastern European states *saisonstaats,* (states for a season). They might not last and then where would France look for assistance, given the Anglo-American attitude? France's small eastern

European allies could never have been a really adequate replacement for the solid pre-war alliance with Russia. In this sense, France's post-war eastern strategy attempted to replace the irreplaceable, but the French tried to convince themselves and the Germans that their new alliances would preserve the status quo.

3 Briand and Appeasement

Coercion failed in the early 1920s and was abandoned after 1924 in favour of *apaisement* (appeasement). This new policy, based largely on the achievement of Franco-German friendship, is usually associated with Aristide Briand who was French Foreign Minister for most of the period between 1924 and 1929. It should be remembered that this was a policy which coincided with the public mood, by now overwhelmingly pacific, and it is therefore possibly misleading totally to identify Briand with conciliation and Poincaré with coercion. Similarly the use of the word appeasement should also induce caution. Briand's policy in the late 1920s involved making concessions from strength, not from weakness, as was the case in the 1930s.

At the time, certainly, the association of Briand with conciliation owed something to his much more attractive personality. Whereas Poincaré was not, in the words of a leading British Foreign Office Official, 'our sort of Frog', Briand was respected across the Channel. He had great charm, eloquence and imagination, and this enabled him to build up a crucial friendship with Gustav Stresemann who was the German Foreign Minister from 1924 until his death in 1929. Together these two men, and to a lesser extent Austen Chamberlain (British Foreign Secretary 1924-9), appeared to put France, Germany and Europe on a new path to peace and understanding.

The first and most memorable product of Briand's new policy was the Treaty of Locarno which was signed by France and Germany in 1925 with Britain and Italy as guarantor powers. Under its terms Germany accepted its existing frontiers with France and Belgium and the existence of the demilitarised zone in the Rhineland. Most significantly, she did so voluntarily.

Treaty of Versailles (Part III Section III)

Article 42   Germany is forbidden to maintain or construct any fortifications either on the left bank of the Rhine or on the right bank to the west of a line drawn 50 kilometres to the east of the Rhine.

Article 43   In the area defined above, the maintenance and the assembly of armed forces either permanently or temporarily, and military manoeuvres of any kind, as well as the upkeep of all permanent works of mobilization, are in the same way forbidden.

Treaty of Locarno

Article 1   The high contracting parties collectively and severally guarantee ... the observance of the stipulations of Articles 42 and 43 of the said Treaty [Versailles] concerning the demilitarized zone.

Article 2   Germany and Belgium, and also Germany and France, mutually undertake that they will not attack or invade each other or resort to war against each other.

This stipulation shall not, however, apply in the case of:-

1. The exercise of legitimate defence, that is to say, resistance to a violation of the undertaking contained in the previous paragraph or a flagrant breach of Articles 42 and 43 of the said Treaty of Versailles, if such breach constitutes an unprovoked act of aggression and by reason of the assembly of armed forces in the demilitarized zone immediate action is necessary.

At Versailles Germany had obviously signed under duress. Briand himself was later to say of Locarno, 'At Locarno we spoke European. It is a new language which one would do well to learn.' They were brave words, but Locarno was fatally flawed from both a European and a French point of view. This was because the Treaty said nothing about the frontiers of France's East European allies. Did Briand perhaps fail to perceive that Stresemann, for all his goodwill, was still a German nationalist and that no German nationalist was going to accept the loss of Danzig and the Polish Corridor? If he did, it was because the euphoria of the moment, which also allowed Germany into the League of Nations in 1926, closed French eyes to the colder reality of German aspirations. They had, in fact, been ignoring evidence of secret and illegal German rearmament for some time.

However, to criticise France for abandoning the coercion of the Poincaré era seems harsh. Briand was merely doing what Britain and the USA had wanted, and Poincaré himself gave his blessing to the new spirit by being present in Geneva when Germany was admitted to the League. Neither was it France's fault that Stresemann was harried to an early grave by nationalist fanatics who could not accept that his policy of detente with the West was in Germany's interest.

The hopes that Briand had raised for Franco-German friendship also proved, all too quickly, to be an illusion. The Kellogg-Briand Pact of 1928 (Kellogg was the American Secretary of State) in which the great powers renounced war as an instrument of policy, and the Young Plan of 1929 which gave Germany until 1988 to pay her reparations, were the last flowerings of the Briand-Stresemann axis (together with France's agreement to pull her troops out of the demilitarised Rhineland in 1930). Briand, too, was to suffer from his nation's ingratitude when, like Clemenceau before him, he was defeated in a presidential election in 1931.

4 Disarmament and Reparations

Throughout the period after Locarno, Franco-German disarmament was on the international agenda but little progress could be made. The French were obsessed by their security, Germany insisted that she be allowed the same level of armaments as France, and even the British were obstructive in the area of naval armaments. So when the Geneva Disarmament Conference finally met in 1932 there was little common ground between the great powers.

The reparations issue continued to poison the atmosphere as well, and Germany had insisted on Allied evacuation of the demilitarised Rhineland before she would even agree to make the reparations payments due from her under the 1924 Dawes Plan. The Hague Conference of 1930 further reduced Germany's payments by one-third, and in 1931 US President Herbert Hoover granted a moratorium of one year in respect of Anglo-French war debts. This was the prelude to the Lausanne Conference of 1932 which cancelled the German reparations altogether in the teeth of French objections. This was actually a recognition that, as a result of the economic slump which hit Europe in the early 1930s, Germany was in no position to pay them. France retaliated by failing to make her debt payments to the USA in 1932.

However, the end of reparations did not materially improve Franco-German relations. Apart from the disarmament issue, further antagonism had been created by the French decision to veto a suggested Austro-German customs union (Anschluss) in 1931 which would, in fact, have been in breach of Article 80 of the Treaty of Versailles. This banned such a union. All this was a great disappointment to Briand who had already conceded much to the Germans. In a desperate attempt to maintain the impetus of the 1920s, the ageing foreign minister had even proposed the idea of a Franco-German customs union, to be followed by a European federal union, but the times were out of joint for such a venture, and Briand himself died in January 1932.

5 The Nazi Threat

Adolf Hitler became German Chancellor on 30 January 1933. In retrospect, this seems to have been a decisive watershed in inter-war French foreign policy. Yet at the time it was not seen in this light. Few Frenchmen had even read *Mein Kampf* (in which Hitler's aggressive foreign policy aims were paraded for all to see), and in France, Hitler seemed only to be the latest crude manifestation of German nationalism. But indications of what was in store for France were given when Hitler walked out of the Geneva Disarmament Conference in the autumn of 1933 after claiming (predictably) that Germany was being unfairly treated. Nevertheless, in the early years of Hitlerism, even the Socialists and Communists in France did not perceive the gravity of the threat.

6 An 'Eastern Locarno'?

The fact that the French government did not have a clear perception of the threat from National Socialist Germany was underlined by the way in which it stuck grimly to the task of trying to establish a so-called 'Four Power Pact' between December 1932 and January 1934. The idea was to bring France, Italy, Britain and Germany together to guarantee the peace of Europe, by making use of Mussolini's known anxiety about the rise of Hitler, a rival fascist dictator, who might bring about an Austro-German Anschluss. Hitler rejected this, just as he had walked out of the League of Nations.

Another French option was an alliance with the USSR, once the Soviet Union had reclaimed a degree of international respectability by being allowed to enter the League of Nations in 1934. But the then French Foreign Minister, Louis Barthou, usually regarded by historians as an anti-German hardliner of the old Poincaré school, realised that the support of the French Right would be needed before any pact could be signed with the USSR. To allay any opposition from that source, Barthou, therefore, proposed a wider settlement, sometimes called an 'Eastern Locarno', which would create mutual assistance treaties between Germany, Poland, Czechoslovakia, the USSR, Finland and the Baltic States. These treaties, like those inspired by France in the 1920s, were to be tied to the League of Nations Covenant.

Whether Barthou's Eastern Locarno could ever have worked is doubtful, particularly in the context of German-Polish antagonism about the Polish Corridor. As it was, in October 1934 Barthou, together with King Alexander of Yugoslavia, was assassinated at Marseilles by a Macedonian terrorist almost certainly in the pay of Mussolini who was trying to destabilise the Yugoslav kingdom. Barthou's death may have marked a major turning point in France's inter-war history by taking from the scene the one leader who had the toughness to stand up to Hitler. The British politician Anthony Eden was to write decades later in his memoirs that the double assassinations at Marseilles marked 'the opening shots of the Second World War'.

Barthou saw clearly that the Treaty of Locarno was as far as Britain would go in any commitment to France, but the historian Anthony Adamthwaite has questioned the traditional emphasis on his anti-Germanism and desire for a Soviet alliance. Barthou, he points out, was under pressure from French military leaders who disliked the idea of a

Soviet alliance and any concession to Germany on disarmament. But Adamthwaite credits him with the effort to 'shore up the crumbling defences' of French diplomacy.

7 Defence Policy

In the 1920s French defence thinking was dominated by offensive tactics and there was, for example, a French plan to deal with a possible German seizure of the Saar coalfield. We have seen how the French were prepared to mount a police action in the Ruhr in 1923. According to the traditional view, France's defence thinking changed dramatically in the 1930s when an immense static line of fortifications, named after the then French Defence Minister, André Maginot, was constructed along the Franco-German frontier. The Maginot Line, with its great guns, concrete bunkers and underground railways, was one of the technological marvels of the world, but it has been held up to ridicule as the classic example of obsolete military thinking. How, many historians have asked, could the French army which had buried itself in costly concrete (the Maginot Line cost hundreds of millions of francs) in the West, hope to help its small allies in the East - those same allies which French statesmen had taken so much time to cultivate?

Modern research suggests that this viewpoint is too simplistic. True, the French probably devoted too much time to thinking about their own defences and not enough time to considering those of their weaker allies, but the change in strategy between the 1920s and 1930s was more gradual than has frequently been suggested. Martin Alexander, in particular, has emphasised how the Maginot strategy was not, as usually alleged, purely defensive but did provide for an offensive phase. According to the plan, Germany would be worn down by a war of blockade and attrition, and then the French army would sally forth from behind its defences and launch the decisive attack. In the light of the rather shaky German economic situation in the late 1930s, such a scenario was not as absurd as it may seem. Germany did suffer from chronic shortages of raw materials, and Britain and France had the naval power to blockade her coastline as they had done during the First World War.

8 The 'New' Appeasement

France's defensive military strategy was wedded to a perceptible change in the conduct of her foreign policy. This is associated with Barthou's successor as Foreign Minister, Pierre Laval, whose policy can be described as 'new' appeasement because it took as its major premise the assumption that France was weaker than Germany and must, therefore, negotiate with her. This contrasted with Briandism in the 1920s when

France was in the stronger position.

Laval has sometimes been thought of as a sinister figure who was soiled by intrigue and his struggle to acquire personal wealth, but he was essentially a pragmatist who had also become a pacifist. Because he was fearful of Italy as well as Germany, Laval also devoted much effort to establishing good relations with Mussolini, just as Barthou had done.

a) Ethiopia

Franco-Italian relations were about to enter a crucial phase. In 1934 Mussolini had threatened to use his army to prevent a Nazi seizure of power in Austria, and in 1935 the Stresa Conference (attended by Britain, France and Italy) produced an agreement about common action if Hitler supported a further coup attempt in Austria.

This seemed encouraging for France, but it was only so in the short term, as Stresa was to prove the high-water mark for co-operation between Mussolini and the western democracies. This was because Mussolini had his eye on the ancient independent African kingdom of Ethiopia where the Italians had suffered a severe military reverse in 1896. Like most Italians, Mussolini felt that Italy's territorial claims had largely been ignored at Versailles, and that she was entitled to a more extensive colonial empire (the existing one was limited to Libya and Italian Somaliland). At Stresa Mussolini had made some generalised remarks about Ethiopia, and came to believe that there would be no Anglo-French objection to Italian annexation of the country. This impression was certainly correct as far as Laval was concerned. He believed that an Italian alliance was worth a colony or two. He also had the support of the French generals who were worried about the possibility that a hostile Italy would force them to post large forces along the Franco-Italian frontier. This would weaken the forces available to face Germany.

Laval claimed to have been taken by surprise when Mussolini attacked Ethiopia in October 1935 and denied encouraging him to do so. Nevertheless, he was anxious to placate Mussolini and tried to bring the British around to his way of thinking. An opportunity seemed to arise when the British Foreign Secretary, Samuel Hoare, visited Paris en route to a holiday in Switzerland in December 1935. He and Laval agreed that Mussolini should be given two-thirds of Ethiopia, but news of this agreement was leaked prematurely by the French press. Once the news got out, British public opinion, outraged by Italian atrocities in Ethiopia, was extremely hostile, and the British government had to disavow Hoare and the pact.

The Hoare-Laval pact undoubtedly damaged Anglo-French relations, as the British believed that they had somehow been deceived by Laval. There was also a division of view about how to deal with Mussolini, for while Britain supported the League's imposition of oil sanctions on Italy, France flatly refused to do so. This may have been because the French were angered by an earlier unilateral British decision in June 1935 to sign the Anglo-German Naval Treaty which allowed Germany to build up to 35 per cent of Royal Navy strength. The French had not been consulted beforehand, and such British behaviour encouraged those who believed that a Soviet or an Italian alliance would give France greater security.

In Whitehall, meantime, Laval was regarded as a trickster, and this view of him persisted for some decades until more recent historical studies portrayed him more favourably as an able statesman, anxious to use Italy as a counterweight to Germany. But, unfortunately for Laval, Mussolini was outraged by the collapse of the Hoare-Laval pact, while the oil sanctions policy was an inglorious fiasco and did not prevent Mussolini completing the conquest of Ethiopia in 1936. The net result of Anglo-French squabbling was that Italy moved closer to the alignment with the Germans which France so dreaded.

b) The Soviet Alliance

Laval's enthusiasm for the Italian alliance was balanced by his lack of enthusiasm, if not outright hostility, to a Soviet alliance. In this he reflected the ideological hostility of France's right-wing parties to Communism both in France and abroad, but a Soviet treaty had been bequeathed to Laval by Barthou, and the Foreign Minister gingerly completed negotiations with the Soviet Foreign Minister. A Franco-Soviet pact was signed in May 1935 but it was hedged about with qualifications. There were no Franco-Soviet military staff talks, the Treaty did not cover the Far East as the Russians (anxious about Japan) wanted, and it was not ratified by France until Laval left the Foreign Ministry in April 1936. Laval also took care to play down its significance in talks with the Germans and Italians. It was clear that he gave priority to improving relations with the Axis powers, especially the Italians.

9 The Rhineland Crisis

The status of the demilitarised left bank of the river Rhine was guaranteed both by the Treaties of Versailles and Locarno (as indicated earlier, Allied troops had left the zone in 1930). This status was brazenly infringed by Hitler on 7 March 1936 when German troops entered the zone. It was the first of the German dictator's so-called 'Saturday surprises' - weekend coups which invariably found the French without a government and the members of the British Cabinet on the grouse moors.

This was the situation facing France in 1936 when Hitler's move had to be confronted by the caretaker government of Albert Sarraut, which was in office pending a general election a few weeks later. Creditably, Sarraut seemed prepared to take countermeasures, and he made a forceful broadcast to the nation in response to Hitler's impertinent offer, seeing that he had flagrantly broken the terms of two treaties, of a 25-year Franco-German non-aggression pact. Yet in the end, France did nothing. Why?

Ostensibly, France had all the major cards in her hands. She had her alliances in eastern Europe, where small powers like Czechoslovakia might well have offered assistance had they been called upon to do so. But, although the politicians seemed prepared to react, Hitler had timed his move to coincide with the lead up to a general election, and the caretaker government felt that it lacked the authority to take firm action.

More crucially, France's legal position did not encourage a swift response. Locarno obliged France to consult with her co-signatories before taking action, and Britain was known to be opposed to anything being done. Her attitude was summed up by the peer who said, 'Germany is only going into her own back garden'. The other signatory power, Italy, had blamed France, as well as Britain, for interfering with her war in Ethiopia and for the collapse of the Hoare-Laval pact. She would certainly not support any move against Germany. Lastly, and despite the fact that she had some 90 divisions available, whereas the Germans had only four, France had made no military plan to deal with the contingency. This fact was made clear by the French Commander-in-Chief, while the politicians were aware that the mobilisation of reservists would be unpopular with elections pending. It seems clear, nevertheless, that the primary failure of will was military rather than political. This is because evidence now available shows that the French generals had effectively written off the demilitarised zone before the event. In addition to this, France did not possess the armoured strike force which would have allowed her to make a rapid response. Such action, had it been taken, would have been based on the assumption that the Germans would have retired from the Rhineland with their tails between their legs. But it is now known that there were German plans for a last ditch resistance if the French reacted.

However, there is no doubt that the Rhineland reoccupation did have adverse consequences for France. The loss of the left bank of the Rhine made it very much harder for her army to penetrate into the heart of Germany and help her East European allies (should she choose to do so). France's failure to act also shook the faith of those allies in her. More seriously, France's inaction in March 1936 appears to have influenced Belgium's decision to declare itself neutral in October 1936. The 1920 Franco-Belgian defence treaty, cancelled by this move, was never popular with the Flemish-speaking part of the Belgian population.

But, whatever the Belgian motives, their decision was crucial for it destroyed the assumption of the French generals that they could fight a war against Germany on the soil of a friendly Belgium. It also left them with the dilemma of whether to extend the Maginot Line to the English Channel which would leave Belgium on the wrong side of the French defences. Such an extension would be hideously expensive and, in the event, the line was not extended along the Franco-Belgian frontier. France proceeded on the assumption that she would be summoned to help Belgium if it were attacked by Germany.

March 1936 was a significant signpost on the road to war in 1939. It was traditionally put forward as the great 'turning point' when Hitler could and should have been stopped. The evidence now available, however, suggests that political and military factors ruled out any decisive French response to Hitler's illegal act even before the remilitarisation took place. Neither, remembering 1923, were the French prepared to act alone against Germany. Naively perhaps but understandably, the French hoped that Hitler's offer of peace in the non-aggression pact was genuine, even if it was accompanied by an impertinent denunciation of the 1935 Franco-Soviet Treaty which Hitler claimed was not compatible with Locarno.

Meeting of the French Service Chiefs, 8 March 1936:

1 GAMELIN: The Government has asked me, 'Are you prepared to hold them?' I replied that, if a conflict between Germany and France were limited to the land front on the Franco-German border, forces on each side would be so large that saturation point 5 would quickly be reached. The fronts would become stabilised. Only the air forces would be able to carry out offensive action on enemy territory. If the theatre of operations extends into Belgium, what will England do?

ADMIRAL DURAND-VIEL: According to the discussions which 10 took place last night at the Foreign Ministry ... the French government, after bringing the question before the Council of the League, will ask that the League should send a commission of enquiry into the Rhineland. Germany would be declared an aggressor. So that it can examine what our attitude will be then, the 15 government has asked the military, 'Are you prepared to drive the Germans out of the zone?'

GAMELIN: By the fact of our entry into the zone, war would be unleashed. Such action would thus require general mobilisation.

Before the Franco-Soviet pact was ratified, General Gamelin gave 20 his written opinion on the probable consequences of this ratification.

---

10 Spain

In July 1936 civil war broke out in Spain between the Republicans and the Nationalist rebels and the outbreak of this war coincided almost exactly with the arrival in power of Léon Blum's Popular Front government (see page 47). All Blum's natural sympathies lay with the Spanish Republic, now under attack from fascist and reactionary forces supported by Nazi Germany and Fascist Italy. But he was mindful of the profound Left-Right divisions in France which probably would be made sharper if the government announced outright support for the Republic. Some French aid did get through to the Republicans, but Blum allowed himself to be persuaded by the British to support a rather shoddy policy known as 'Non-intervention'. This involved not supporting either side despite the farcical adhesion to the agreement of Germany and Italy, who were openly helping the Nationalist rebels.

As it was, Blum's non-interventionist stance caused trouble with the French Communist Party, which helped to bring down the Popular Front in 1937 (see page 49). But he was almost certainly right in identifying Germany as the major danger to France (Hitler delighted in attacking both Blum's Jewishness and his Socialism). Non-intervention, however, led inevitably to the defeat of the Spanish Republic, and no foreign policy issue perhaps showed the influence of French domestic politics more strongly than the Spanish war.

11 The Anschluss

In 1931 France had obstructed the proposed Austro-German Anschluss, but by 1938 the international situation had markedly altered. Most importantly, Mussolini, who had protected Austrian independence in 1934, now regarded Austria as 'a German problem'.

French statesmen were aware of the danger to Austrian independence from Germany, but as over the Rhineland, they would not move without British support. Documentary evidence shows that France did try to concert action with Britain over Austria in 1937, but faced with British disinterest, Prime Minister Chautemps told the American ambassador that he could see 'no way to prevent Hitler swallowing Austria'. This Hitler duly did over the weekend of 11-12 March 1938, and France contented itself with a diplomatic protest. Given the fact that not for a moment did the French consider going to the aid of the unfortunate Austrian Chancellor, was it likely that they would help those states with which they had a formal alliance?

12 The Czech Crisis

The Treaty of Saint Germain in 1919 which dismantled the old Austro-

Hungarian Empire had also created the new state of Czechoslovakia. But the Czechoslovak Republic, although it contained a majority of Czechs and Slovaks, also had a three-million strong German minority living in the western frontier area known as the Sudentenland.

The Czech government did not treat its racial minorities badly, but the Sudeten Germans had suffered severely during the 1930s depression, creating resentments which found expression through a Sudeten German Party led by Konrad Henlein. Henlein's demand in the first instance was for self-government for the Sudeten Germans inside the Czech Republic, but it is now known that from 1933 onwards, the Sudeten German Party was concerting its actions with Berlin. After the Austrian Anschluss in March 1938, Sudeten German demands for autonomy became more and more strident. So did Hitler's verbal attacks on the Czech government of Dr Eduard Benes, which was accused of atrocities against the German minority.

The French position in the event of an open attack by Germany on Czechoslovakia seemed clearcut. The agreement of 1924 with its rather vague military provisions had been replaced by the 1935 Franco-Czech Treaty which pledged France to help the Czechs if they were attacked, and placed the same obligation on them if France were attacked. A similar treaty, also signed in 1935, bound the USSR and Czechoslovakia together but with an important proviso. Only if France honoured her promise to help the Czechs first, would the Russians help Czechoslovakia against an aggressor state. This reservation was to loom large over the Czech crisis of May-September 1938.

At the outset of the crisis it did indeed seem that France would honour her obligations. In the third week in May the Czech government mobilised its army (one of the best equipped in Europe) in response to rumours that Germany was about to attack. France then stated that she would stand by her treaty with Czechoslovakia, as did the USSR. Crucially, too, Britain stated that if France were involved in a war to defend Czechoslovakia, she might also feel compelled to intervene.

Such a display of unity against Hitler seemed impressive. Yet the major significance of the 'May Scare' for historians has been that it enraged Hitler (who had actually not been planning to attack the Czechs) and made him determined to 'smash Czechoslovakia'. Less noted has been its impact in France where the shock of an imminent conflict made the Daladier government even more anxious to avoid war. This accounts for an increasing French tendency to follow the British lead during the Czech crisis, although it was France and not Britain which had the alliance with the Czechs.

As Hitler's verbal attacks on the Czech government grew more strident in the late summer of 1938, the British Prime Minister, Neville Chamberlain, and not Daladier, took the lead in negotiations with Germany. In August and September Chamberlain dominated, first sending his own observer to the Sudetenland, and then meeting Hitler personally at Berchtesgaden (15 September) and Godesburg (22 September). The French were merely kept informed.

Why did the French government appear to absolve itself of responsibility in this way? One reason was that France was obsessed with the need for the British alliance, without which its government was convinced it could do nothing. Linked with this anxiety about Britain was distrust of the USSR, sharpened by the knowledge that Stalin had probably damaged the fighting effectiveness of the Red Army in his 1937 purge of its officer corps. (However, recent research suggests that Stalin would have helped the Czechs if France had done so.) By 1938 the vehemence of the anti-Communist and anti-Socialist Right in France had reached fever pitch with slogans such as 'Better Hitler than Blum'. This political division was sharply reflected by the French press. For example, one newspaper demanded to know why it was necessary for Frenchmen to die to preserve the domination of six million Czechs over three million Germans.

The government was also fatally divided. Daladier was clearly aware of France's obligation to the Czechs even if he allowed Chamberlain to bully them into making concessions to Germany, whereas Bonnet, his Foreign Minister, wanted Britain to take the lead so that he could shift the odium for selling out the Czechs on to her. Bonnet's influence was consistently negative and defeatist in the Czech crisis, but there were those like Mandel and Reynaud, the so-called *bellicistes* (hawks), who wanted to stand by the Czechs.

Neither was the resolve of the politicians strengthened by the advice they received from the military. The Commander-in-Chief, Gamelin, would do nothing without the British, and in the vital area of air power, France was very badly served. The air force commander visited German aircraft factories in 1938 and returned in terror, remarking that if war should come the French air force would be shot out of the sky 'within a fortnight' - actually, he had been duped into believing that aircraft prototypes were examples of mass production.

However, even allowing for these divisions, there appeared to be some strengthening of the French position over Czechoslovakia. When Chamberlain went to Godesburg on 22 September, Hitler demanded evacuation of the entire Sudetenland by the Czechs by 1 October and Daladier regarded this as unacceptable. At this point war seemed inevitable and French troops manned the Maginot Line. French public opinion also seemed to accept the inevitability of war, so that a German diplomat reported that 'the population is growing accustomed to the idea of war'.

a) The Munich Conference

Suddenly, however, on 28 September Hitler invited Chamberlain, Daladier and Mussolini to meet him to discuss the Sudeten question.

But Hitler's decision to convene the conference at the eleventh hour must have been influenced by the knowledge that the French government would go to the very limits of concession to preserve the peace.

The Munich Conference was duly convened (with Mussolini, unknown to Chamberlain and Daladier, working hand-in-glove with Hitler) but there was minimal discussion. The Czechs were forced to cede the Sudetenland under pressure from Britain and France without their representatives even being allowed into the meeting of the four powers. The betrayal of this small democratic state, France's most faithful ally in eastern Europe, was well expressed in a Czech poem. 'Sweet France, Proud Albion,' it ran, 'and we loved you'.

Unlike his British colleague, Daladier felt the shame of the occasion. He had appeared to offer support to the Czechs but, because of personal weakness and because he presided over a divided Cabinet and nation, he allowed his signature to be appended to the Munich Agreement. It can, of course, be argued in Daladier's defence that given the negative input from the military, he had little option but to do so. At one point the Prime Minister asked Gamelin whether it would be possible to fight for Czechoslovakia, and was told that it would need another Somme-style battle. Daladier never raised the issue with his Commander-in-Chief again.

On his return to Paris, therefore, Daladier had few illusions. He was all the more astonished then when, turning up his raincoat collar against the expected volleys of rotten tomatoes, he was greeted like a popular hero. 'The poor fools, the poor fools,' Daladier is alleged to have remarked to a colleague.

b) The Results of Munich

There can be no doubt that France was a clear loser from the Munich Agreement. Her Czech ally had been gravely weakened by the loss of its frontier defences, and French failure to honour treaty obligations produced suspicion in Moscow. It is clear that after Munich Stalin, fearing a western deal with Hitler against the USSR, began considering an accommodation of his own with Nazi Germany. In France itself Munich was denounced by the PCF which gave Daladier an excuse to begin a strong anti-Communist campaign, but outside the appeasement circles frequented by Bonnet there were few illusions. Nevertheless, modern historians have argued that the choices open to France were limited. Richard Overy, for example, argues that while from the French viewpoint the Munich settlement 'was not an honourable one ... it was an understandable one'. Understandable because France was weak in the air (although not as weak as her airforce chief thought), and aware that Britain would not fight for the Sudetenland. A more desperate hope was for American assistance, but it was killed off in President

Roosevelt's two-word telegram of approval to Chamberlain at the time of Munich, reading 'Good man'.

Should France have fought in September 1938 as her Czech allies were willing to do, with the possibility of Soviet aid? Perhaps, but the argument is a finely balanced one.

c) After Munich

There was a discernible toughening up in French foreign policy after the Munich Conference, particularly in the area of Franco-Italian relations where Laval had tried so hard to woo the Italian dictator. His failure was underlined by the vociferous Italian demands in the winter of 1938-9 for Nice (formerly Italian) and concessions by France in North Africa. However, France completely refused to concede anything to Italy and strengthened the fortifications along the Franco-Italian frontier. Her generals were convinced that the Italians, at least, could be seen off.

Ironically, this French toughness put new strains on the Anglo-French alliance, for Chamberlain continued to hope, as the French had done in the mid-1930s, that Mussolini could be utilised as a counterweight to Hitler. France's toughness towards Italy sizeably reduced such hopes and so displeased Britain.

Bonnet continued to hope for good relations with Germany, and a rather meaningless Franco-German accord was signed in December 1938, with hopes of strengthening trade links. But such hopes for a general improvement in the state of Franco-German relations were rudely shattered by Hitler's occupation of the rest of the Czech lands on 15 March 1939 and by the subsequent detachment of Slovakia as a German puppet state. Daladier at least seemed to see this as final evidence of German perfidy. He had continually pressed the British to introduce conscription after Munich, and he finally got his way in March 1939. Rearmament was stepped up in France, and there were large purchases of aircraft from the USA.

Did this mean the end of appeasement in France? Only to a limited extent, it seems, as Bonnet remained Foreign Minister and while he was in post he resisted the prospect of war. This strange schizophrenia in French policy persisted because Daladier, fearful of the Foreign Minister's political allies, dared not sack him. Nevertheless, Daladier's more assertive policy seemed to prosper when France got the staff talks with the British for which she had asked for so long, and an Anglo-Polish alliance was signed in April 1939.

13 The Polish Crisis and War

Predictably, after dismembering Czechoslovakia, Hitler began to demand the return of the port of Danzig (under League of Nations' control) and the Polish Corridor. It was only at this point that the Franco-British side belatedly saw the importance of the Soviet alliance, although it must be admitted that even then the French were keener than the British. But they both thought that Hitler might moderate his behaviour if faced with the prospect of an alliance between France, Britain and the USSR.

In fact, the opportunity had virtually gone. Stalin had already put out feelers to Germany, and in May 1939 he removed Litvinov, the Foreign Minister, who was firmly associated with collective security and the French alliance, and replaced him with his own henchman, Molotov. A Franco-British delegation was sent to Moscow, but negotiations stalled once again on the vital question of transit rights for the Red Army in Poland and Romania. The Romanians might tolerate such access but the Poles adamantly refused to do so, just as they refused to budge over the question of Danzig and the Polish Corridor.

Daladier was desperate for a Soviet alliance at this stage, and even told the Russians (falsely) that Poland had agreed to the stationing of Red Army troops on its soil. Then all the negotiations were rendered redundant by Stalin's sudden, but not unforeseeable decision to sign a non-aggression pact with Germany on 23 August. This Nazi-Soviet Pact freed Hitler from the fear of Soviet intervention should he decide to invade Poland. This he duly did on 1 September. Even at this stage Bonnet made undignified efforts to secure Italian mediation, and there was typical Franco-British discord about the timing of a declaration of war on Germany. For once, however, this was a result of strains within the British Cabinet rather than of disagreements between the soon-to-be allies. It arose because colleagues of Chamberlain, outraged by attempts to avoid war yet again at the eleventh hour, insisted that Britain declare war six hours before France. Gamelin had insisted on the need for extra time to evacuate children from Paris, before the declaration of war came at 5 pm on 3 September. France entered the war in a sombre but realistic mood.

14 A Nation Renewed?

Recent historical research has stressed the fact that France in 1938-9 (post-Munich) was in an altogether more vigorous mood. This contradicts the traditional view that throughout the period from 1936 to 1939 the French lamely tagged along behind Britain. This interpretation was particularly associated with A.J.P. Taylor who accused French statesmen of 'wriggling' and 'dodging' in their anxiety to avoid war at all costs.

This thesis does retain its validity up to Munich, but thereafter opinion polls, a vigorous policy towards Italy and the increasing pace of rearmament back the view that there was a new public and political mood in France. This was accelerated by the sharp improvement in the

French economy (see page 51). Among a new revisionist school of historians, the American Robert Young has accused Taylor of 'cultural bias' in dismissing France's recovery after Munich. Confusingly, perhaps, French historians like Jean Baptiste Duroselle and René Girault have continued to identify a mood of national defeatism! None though have attempted to refute the extent of the economic recovery which fuelled France's rearmament programme.

15 Colonial Policy

France had an extensive colonial empire, most significantly in Africa, the Middle East, but also in Asia where she had to be aware of a potential Japanese threat to French Indo-China.

In the inter-war period colonial difficulties centred on Africa and the Middle East, notably in Morocco and Syria. In Morocco, the French Resident-General, Marshal Lyautey (1912-25), encouraged European settlement which had risen to 130,000 by the 1930s. This, in turn, may have encouraged the revolt of the Berber chieftain, Abd-el-Krim, between 1921 and 1926, although Italian meddling was almost certainly a factor.

More seriously, Syria, a French mandate under the League of Nations, revolted against French rule in 1925. Damascus had to be bombarded by French troops but the revolt dragged on until 1936 when the Syrians were promised eventual independence.

Contemporary newsreels showed a powerful, confident French empire, while ignoring the ominous rise in African and Asian nationalism in the 1930s which would eventually bring it down.

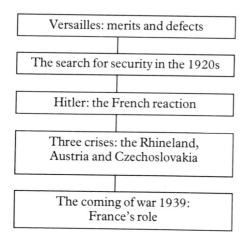

Versailles: merits and defects

The search for security in the 1920s

Hitler: the French reaction

Three crises: the Rhineland, Austria and Czechoslovakia

The coming of war 1939: France's role

Summary - The Search for Security, 1919-39

Making notes on *'The Search for Security 1918-39'*

This chapter has dealt with the role of France as a great power in the inter-war period, an era of special complexity in international affairs. Good sub-headings are, therefore, invaluable in your notes and the following are suggested:
1   France and the Versailles Settlement.
1.1 The clauses as they affected France.
1.2 French expectations.
1.3 France as the guardian of the settlement.
1.4 Poincaré and coercion.
2   Franco-German detente.
2.1 The partnership of Briand and Stresemann.
2.2 Locarno and its significance.
2.3 The Kellogg Pact and the Young Plan.
3   The Search for Security 1929-35.
3.1 Disarmament and the end of reparations.
3.2 France's reaction to Hitler's coming to power.
3.3 Barthou and an 'Eastern Locarno'.
3.4 The move to appeasement.
4   France and the Major Crises.
4.1 The Rhineland.
4.2 The Anschluss.
4.3 The Czech crisis.
5   France and the Outbreak of the Second World War.
5.1 Franco-Italian relations.
5.2 The Polish Crisis.
5.3 French policy to the outbreak of war.

Answering essay questions on *'The Search for Security 1918-39'*

Examiners are likely to set two sorts of question related to France's inter-war foreign policy. Some will focus on the post-war settlement of 1919, others will concentrate on the origins of the Second World War. It is unlikely that many will highlight a specifically French role, so anything that you have read in this chapter is likely to tie in with the companion *Access to History* volumes about British inter-war foreign policy and international relations as a whole. Study the following questions, which are in fact restricted to French foreign policy alone.

1   'Too lenient in its severity.' Discuss the view that the Versailles Treaty was in fact too lenient to provide France with real security.
2   Why did Briand adopt a policy of detente towards Germany in the 1920s and why did this policy ultimately fail?

3   In what sense could it be said that France's inter-war defence aims were incompatible?

4   Why did the French government fail to make an armed response to Hitler's remilitarisation of the Rhineland in 1936, and what were the consequences of this decision?

5   Discuss the view that from the French perspective the Munich settlement if 'not an honourable one ... was an understandable one'.

6   Assess France's responsibility for the outbreak of the Second World War in September 1939.

Questions 1 and 5 contain quotations and students sometimes find this sort of question daunting. However, there is no reason for you to be intimidated if you have prepared thoroughly. But you will need to ensure that you understand the point the quote is making. Question 1 is particularly teasing in this respect. A list of severe and lenient aspects might help. Terminology is also important in answering questions. You cannot really answer Question 2 unless you understand what detente means. At best, a largely irrelevant narrative style essay would result. Note also the likely overlap with the material in Chapter 3. This would be especially true in Question 1.

Source-based questions on 'The Search for Security 1918-39'

1 The Treaties of Versailles and Locarno

Study the extracts on pages 60 and 61. Answer the following questions:

a)   What phrase is normally used to describe the area mentioned in Articles 42 and 43 of the Versailles Treaty? (2 marks)

b)   Who were the 'high contracting parties' mentioned in Article 1 of the Treaty of Locarno? (2 marks)

c)   In what way does Article 2 of the Locarno Treaty contrast with the extracts quoted from the Versailles Treaty? (5 marks)

d)   Using the material available in the extracts, show how French attitudes towards Germany had changed between 1919 and 1925. (6 marks)

CHAPTER 5

The Fall of France and the Vichy Regime

1 The Phoney War

France went to war in September 1939 reluctantly. The spirit was quite different from that of 1914. Then the war had been a great cause to save the homeland from German aggression, but in 1939 the slogan was 'let's get it over with'. This lack of enthusiasm was reflected in France's response to the plight of her ally Poland on whose behalf she had gone to war in the first place. The Franco-Polish military agreement of May 1939 said that France would attack Germany within 15 days of the mobilisation of her army. She kept this promise, just. A small French force advanced into the Saarland, and occupied 20 villages. The guns of the great Maginot Line fired a few shells. Then, after Poland had been defeated, the French Commander-in-Chief, Gamelin, pulled his men back, secretly relieved that the Germans had not counter-attacked from behind their Siegfried Line. The German generals were amazed that the French had not taken advantage of their involvement in Poland. They knew that the Siegfried Line was both incomplete and thinly defended.

At home there was confusion. The French mobilisation was too all-embracing and actually called up skilled workers (such as those in armaments factories) who were needed for the war effort. These men soon had to be sent home. At the same time, the politicians were not committed to all-out war. Daladier, the French Prime Minister, and Reynaud, his Finance Minister, remembered the First World War and its aftermath. They felt that France's economic effort had not been fairly rewarded in the peace treaty. So Daladier wanted above all to preserve a sound economy and refused to set up a Ministry of Munitions. Plans for rationing were also opposed by the Ministry of Agriculture. This desire to avoid crippling France's economy was also linked to the Anglo-French belief that the German economy was shaky. It was thought that a blockade like the one used in the First World War would bring Germany to her knees. Britain and France had the naval power to mount such a blockade. After the French 'mini-offensive' life soon returned to normal in what the Americans called 'the phoney war' (the French phrase is *drôle de guerre* or 'joke war'). This expression was coined to describe the curious state of no peace, no war, on the western front between the collapse of Poland and the summer of 1940.

Evacuated Parisians returned to Paris and the night clubs and restaurants reopened. The great French singer Maurice Chevalier recorded 'Paris will always be Paris'. It was hard to remember there was a war on. Meantime, there was the usual feuding in the French government. Daladier and Reynaud detested one another but the government needed Reynaud's financial expertise to try to win the war.

Further problems were created by the attitude of the sizeable French communist party which had been instructed by Stalin to oppose the war following the Nazi-Soviet Pact of August 1939. There was evidence of communist sabotage in tank and aircraft factories, but Daladier probably made a serious error in banning the party and persecuting its membership which merely went underground. Even more foolishly, quite harmless anti-Nazi refugees of German and Austrian origin were put in internment camps and badly treated. There was a general suspicion of foreigners which also vented itself on those traditional scapegoats, the Jews. Even before the war started foreign Jewish immigrants had been harassed by not being given permanent residence permits. Instead, they had to get temporary permits, renewed weekly. After the outbreak of war attacks on Jews in the extreme right-wing press were increased but the government did nothing about them, despite their obvious fascist overtones. The contrast with the treatment of communists was glaring.

However, the most disastrous effect of the *drôle de guerre* was on the French army. A variety of factors combined to make the inactivity of this seven-month period far more harmful to the French than to the Germans. First, the winter of 1939-40 was the worst in living memory and this prevented the French from carrying out crucial work on the fortifications along the Franco-Belgian border to the north of the Maginot Line. Second, conditions in the French army were very unsatisfactory. Pay for non-commissioned ranks was poor and the officers were both uninterested in their men and far better off in every way. The soldiers in the Maginot forts, with their compulsory sunlamp treatment and underground bunkers, were at least warm in that awful winter, but they faced a common enemy - *ennui* (boredom). The odd shot was fired off at the Germans, but much time was spent playing football and painting barracks.

'French leave' or taking long weekends off became commonplace, as did drunkenness. Special rooms had to be set aside at railway stations where soldiers could recover from their hangovers! These were symptoms of a disintegrating morale which should have been picked up by the high command. German propaganda was also skilful in working on French grievances. A favourite ploy was to tell French soldiers that while they were at the front, their British allies were making off with their girlfriends and wives. As the British were never popular in France, this was readily believed. Frenchmen pointed out, not unreasonably, that the BEF (British Expeditionary Force) consisted of just 5 divisions while France had 90 divisions in the field.

Generally, the *drôle de guerre* could do little good to an army which was unenthusiastic about going to war in the first place. But there is a difference between lack of enthusiasm and not wanting to fight at all, and modern research has refuted the idea that the French army was riddled with defeatism. The air force was a cause of far more serious concern. The French government was terrified of provoking German air raids and banned attacks on Germany. It would not even let the RAF bomb Germany from airfields in France. However, it has to be admitted that the British government was equally timid. Instead, the Allies resorted to 'confetti warfare', dropping leaflets telling the Germans they were bound to lose the war. Another feature of this waiting strategy was a penchant for 'side-shows'. They had the great virtue of keeping hostilities off French soil. A scheme was concocted to land Allied troops at the Greek port of Salonika with the aim of linking up with the Yugoslavs who were not even in the war at that stage.

Another provided for the bombing of Soviet oilfields in the Caucasus from French Syria, with the object of stopping Germany getting oil from that source. This crazy idea was put forward when Soviet Russia attacked Finland in the winter of 1939-40. Immediately there was great enthusiasm for helping Finland in France, although this would have involved her being at war with Russia and Germany at the same time. The British were equally enthusiastic, but fortunately for the Allies, Finland surrendered before anything could be done.

The 'sideshow' strategy has often been blamed on the French Commander-in-Chief, Maurice Gamelin, but modern research has shown this charge to be false. Gamelin opposed such white elephants, which resulted from flights of fancy by politicians like Daladier, and his own arch rival, General Weygand.

When Finland surrendered in March 1940 its end did, rather absurdly, bring down the Daladier government in France. In reality, the change proved to be merely cosmetic - another example of the endless political musical chairs which were such a feature of the Third Republic. Daladier just became Defence Minister instead, while his rival, Paul Reynaud ('Mickey Mouse' to his enemies) became Prime Minister. Although Reynaud mistrusted both Daladier and Gamelin, he had a majority of only one in Parliament, and could not challenge Daladier's demand that Gamelin keep his job.

2 The Battle of France

Paul Reynaud was a pugnacious leader who was admired by Churchill, and there were others in his government such as the Interior Minister, Mandel, who were also fully committed to the concept of victory over Germany. Reynaud had barely been appointed Prime Minister when the *drôle de guerre* came to an end. In April 1940 Hitler attacked both Denmark and Norway, the former offering only token resistance, and the latter inviting Anglo-French help. The expeditionary force sent there soon had to be withdrawn to face a greater emergency in Western Europe.

The assumption of the French high command was that any German attack in Western Europe would be based on the old Schlieffen Plan of 1914. This assumption was strengthened by a freak accident in January 1940 when a German aircraft crashlanded in Belgium with their invasion plans on board. The plans were passed on to the Allies and did indeed show that the Germans intended to sweep through Belgium, so avoiding the Maginot Line fortifications. What Gamelin and his generals did not know was that after the discovery of the original German plan, Hitler had radically changed his intentions. A new plan formulated by General von Manstein provided for a sweep through both Belgium and Holland, and a thrust by powerful panzer (tank) formations through the heavily wooded Ardennes. On the French side of the River Meuse this area was lightly defended by rather poor quality

German Invasion Plan 1940

divisions. However, it is not true, as is often claimed, that the French had decided that the Ardennes was 'impassable' for tanks. In the 1930s Marshal Pétain had said that it would be impassable for them provided 'special dispositions' were made. Unfortunately for France, her defences in this part of the front remained inadequate. The Germans had also guessed correctly that the Anglo-French response to an attack on Belgium and Holland would involve sending a large part of their forces to help those neutral states. Once this process had begun, the Germans would make their powerful armoured thrust through the Ardennes which the French were not expecting. Events turned out exactly as the Germans had hoped.

Hitler launched his long-expected attack on 10 May 1940 (by coincidence the day that Winston Churchill replaced Neville Chamberlain as British Prime Minister). Gamelin immediately put his own plan to assist Belgium and Holland into operation. His eyes were fixed on the battle north of France's frontiers, whereas they should have been concentrated on the Ardennes which turned out to be the crucial part of the battlefield. The speed and power of the German attack from the Ardennes took the French completely by surprise. Within a few days, the Germans had thrust aside the inadequate French defenders on the Meuse and flooded into the flat plains of Northern France. To the north, panzer divisions smashed through Dutch and Belgian defences and a terrible disaster faced the Allied armies.

The successful German attack through the Ardennes meant that the Anglo-French forces in Belgium and Holland were cut off from the rest of the French army to the south. As early as 15 May Reynaud telephoned Churchill to say 'we have lost the battle'. A crucial factor here was Gamelin's decision to send one of the best French armies, the 7th, to help the Dutch. So when the Germans unexpectedly broke through in the Ardennes he had nothing left with which to make a counter-attack.

In the crisis Reynaud took panic measures. Daladier was shunted over to the Ministry of Foreign Affairs, and Reynaud himself took over the Defence Ministry. Gamelin was sacked and replaced by General Weygand who, at 73 (but like him, a hero of the First World War), was even older than Gamelin. Disastrously, too, the aged defeatist Marshal Pétain, now in his eighties, was brought back from the Madrid embassy and made Reynaud's deputy. Reynaud hoped to rally the nation by bringing back the victor of Verdun, but Pétain's defeatism seeped into the government's bones.

Meanwhile, matters went from bad to worse on the battlefield. Holland had already capitulated, and in late May, the Belgian King Leopold asked for a ceasefire. For this he was most unfairly criticised by the French and British who knew perfectly well that the Belgian army was on the verge of collapse. Worse still, from the French point of view, was the decision made by Lord Gort, the Commander of the BEF, that the British army must save itself. He therefore ordered his men to retreat to the northern French port of Dunkirk from where they would be evacuated by the Royal Navy. There were loud French cries about betrayal when this happened, and it is true that Gort gave the French very little warning of what he was about to do. It is also true that his decision saved the British army from destruction. Allied naval forces evacuated some 300,000 men from the beaches of Dunkirk by the first week of June, including thousands of French, but Dunkirk had sealed the fate of the Allied armies in the north. One point often overlooked by British historians is that the French defenders of Lille gave the BEF time to escape with their gallant defence of the area. This was recognised by the Germans who allowed them to march out with their regimental colours after the surrender of the city.

After their victory in the North, the Germans unleashed their full fury against the outnumbered French forces in the South. To boost their numbers, Weygand released men from the now quite useless Maginot Line - *le trou* or 'the hole' as its defenders called it - and tried to form a front along the River Somme. Although the French fought gallantly, it became increasingly obvious that the end was near. On 9 June the French government was evacuated from Paris to Tours and on 14 June, the Germans entered Paris. A decision had been made to make Paris an 'open city', so it was undefended. Its loss was, of course, a shattering blow to French pride.

Drunken French soldiers surrender in 1940

Even in such adversity, Paul Reynaud wanted to move the civil administration of France to North Africa, while the French army took responsibility for any armistice with the Germans. In this he was strongly encouraged by Churchill who offered to create a sort of 'Anglo-French Union' which would unite the resources of the two nations. France, after all, still had her empire and a sizeable navy, but Reynaud was undermined by the defeatists in his cabinet led by Pétain, who was determined to end the struggle. On 16 June Reynaud resigned from his post as Prime Minister and was succeeded by Pétain. The following day Pétain broadcast to the French people saying that the war was lost and that France must seek an armistice. Only a few Frenchmen dissented from his decision, notably General Charles de Gaulle, the Under-Secretary for War, who fled to England. There, on 18 June, de Gaulle made his famous BBC broadcast calling on his fellow countrymen to continue the struggle against Germany. Few Frenchmen were impressed at the time by this call to arms by a general few of them had heard of. Extracts from the texts of both broadcasts are given below:

1 Frenchmen, at the appeal of the President of the Republic, I have today assumed the direction of the government of France. Convinced of the affection of our admirable army ... convinced of the confidence of the whole nation, I give myself to France to 5 assuage her misfortune ... It is with a heavy heart that I say we must end the fight. Last night I applied to our adversary to ask if he is prepared to seek with me, soldier to soldier, after the battle, honourably, the means whereby hostilities may cease.

1 I, General de Gaulle, at this moment in London, invite French officers and soldiers at present on British territory, engineers, and skilled workers, to get in touch with me.
    Whatever happens, the flame of French resistance must not be 5 quenched. Nor shall it be.

France was granted an armistice after a meeting at Compiégne on 22 June which Hitler, with calculated vindictiveness, insisted on holding in the same railway carriage Marshal Foch had used for the German armistice signing in 1918. Under the armistice terms, northern and western France, including Paris, was to be occupied by the Germans (this included all the richest areas). The rest of France was to remain under Marshal Pétain's administration, the army was to be disarmed and demobilised, and the navy was to be demobilised under German supervision.
    The last point was extremely important to the British who were naturally suspicious of German intentions. In the event, they need not have worried because the French had decided to scuttle their warships rather than let them fall into German hands. However, this was not known to the British government at the time. Unfortunately, the French

did little to assist them. Powerful units of the French fleet lay at anchor in the North African port of Mers-el-Kébir, and the British did not want Germany to gain control of them. A series of confused meetings could not persuade the French to join the British or sail to a neutral port, and so the Royal Navy sank the French ships. Churchill was rightly concerned with the possible threat to British security posed by these ships, but in France, this action was seen to be yet another example of British treachery. Mers-el-Kébir was the low point of the always troubled Anglo-French relationship after 1918.

3 Why France Fell

The fall of France was primarily a result of military defeat. Both at the time and later, attempts were made to link it with Communist sabotage of war industries in 1939-40 and right-wing defeatism. While these were factors in the French defeat, they were not the decisive ones.

There were undoubtedly serious deficiencies in France's armed forces. The French High Command, for example, preferred to use tanks for infantry support rather than as armoured spearheads as the Germans did. These tanks lacked radio sets and could not communicate on the battlefield as their opponents could. The close co-ordination between army and air force, which was such a feature on the German side, was also missing on the French one. There was a strange reluctance to bomb German tank and troop concentrations as they crossed the River Meuse until it was too late.

The lack of decisive leadership was also important. France's generals were old men, at their peak in the First World War, who seemed to be stunned by the sheer speed of the German breakout from the Ardennes. But the Germans did achieve an almost complete strategic surprise. They abandoned the old Schlieffen Plan and lured the Allies into a trap, as Gamelin's 'Dyle Plan' involved sending the best French and Allied troops into Holland and Belgium. He did not realise, until it was too late, that the German attack on those countries was subsidiary. The decisive thrust came through the Ardennes and when it succeeded, the Allied armies were cut in two. France was, therefore, defeated, and defeated in only six weeks. The speed of this defeat makes the old explanations for the disaster an attractive one. The French were poorly led, lacked fighting spirit, and ran away. They were destroyed, it was alleged, by an avalanche of fast-moving German tanks (panzers).

Military strength	Allied	German
Army divisions	136	136
Tanks	3,100	2,400
Aircraft	1,800	3,000

(These figures apply to the number in the field rather than those built.)

All these assertions can now be seriously questioned. It is true that Gamelin was taken aback by the speed of the German advance, but senior German generals had also been sceptical about the value of tanks and initially opposed the Manstein Plan. Indeed they were so angry with him that they ensured that he played no leading part in the Battle of France. The architects of the German victory were supremely confident junior tank commanders, not the High Command. It was also true in 1940 that French tanks were both greater in numbers and superior in design, and that, although second-class troops along the Meuse performed poorly, there were heroic defences, too (like the one at Lille mentioned above). Thus, although there were deficiencies in the French army in 1940, it is clear that there was no overall collapse of morale.

In an important sense, the defeat of 1940 was an Allied defeat, not just a French one. The French were hindered by a lack of co-operation from neutral Belgium and Holland, which meant that their generals did not know as much as they should have done about Belgian and Dutch defences. Britain's contribution to the war effort was not as substantial as it should have been, and the BEF's speedy retreat to Dunkirk with minimal prior warning to the French, opens her to the charge of selfishness. The defeat when it came was largely a result of poor co-ordination, bad planning and mutual backbiting.

But it was by no means inevitable. It is now recognised that the campaign was a much closer run affair than was realised at the time. Hitler remained nervous and edgy throughout, as did his leading generals, fearing a counter-attack which never came. More French resolution may have made this possible, and it is easy to forget that the triumph on the Marne in 1914 had almost been a disaster. Just as in 1914, the Germans in 1940 were on a tight rigorously rehearsed timetable in which a serious delay (for example, at the Meuse crossing points) could have ruined everything.

4 Pétain and the National Revolution

General de Gaulle's appeal attracted very little support anywhere, save in the French colonies of Central Africa. In metropolitan France, the Chamber of Deputies voted by overwhelming majorities to revise the Constitution of the Third Republic, and to vest the leadership of France in the hands of the venerable Philippe Pétain. From the outset, Pétain distanced himself from the Republic by declaring himself '*Chef de l'état français*' (Head of the French State). But there were also distinct monarchical overtones in his use of the phrase 'We Philippe Pétain'. Pétain, like many right-wing army officers, had monarchist sympathies but the phrase was more revealing about the way in which he ruled the Unoccupied Zone of France from the old spa town of Vichy. Far from being senile and the victim of crafty advisers, Pétain was remarkably vigorous for a man of 84. He removed those, like Laval, who seemed to threaten his personal position, and kept in his hands more power than any Frenchman since the days of Napoleon III. A minister gives a good description of him at this time.

1 The Marshal certainly had surprising physical vigour, and was extraordinarily well preserved. He had no loss of facilities, had a spring in his step, read easily without glasses. He had a fine face, a distinguished carriage, above all radiated authority and even a sort
5 of majesty. This undoubted personal magnetism, which was rather formidable, came more from his presence and the glory of his name than from his conversation. Beyond doubt he had extensive knowledge and could form sound opinions on a variety of subjects; but he only really dominated a discussion when it was on matters
10 concerned with the training of military leaders.

From contacts with him over more than two years, I remember two characteristics in particular. In cabinet meetings, when he had let his own feelings be known and nominally questioned one of his ministers on the same subject, you soon felt he was offended if the
15 minister, although putting it with the greatest deference, expressed an opinion which did not agree with his own. I think this was due to the traditions of military discipline. In the army, an officer never has anyone contradicting him.

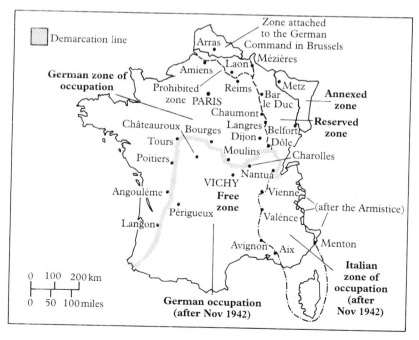

Map showing Vichy and the Occupied zones

Apart from being Commander-in-Chief of the Vichy forces (historians call his regime after its seat of government), Pétain was also responsible for all government appointments, and the passing of all laws. It is clear that he enjoyed the privileges of power. He surrounded himself with sycophantic hangers-on, and encouraged the development of a personality cult. Portraits of 'Le Maréchal' appeared everywhere, and personal tours of Vichy France in the winter of 1940-1 were a huge success. The support of the Catholic Church was an important element in the establishment of Vichy, and a Catholic archbishop described Pétain as the personification of 'suffering France'.

Pétain thus stood for the traditional virtues suggested by the Vichy slogan, 'family, work, country', although his personal life was far from perfect. Right-wingers relied on him to restore the old conservative values of France after the excesses of the Popular Front. They, like the Marshal, were fiercely anti-Communist, and Pétain seems to have genuinely believed that anti-Marxism would provide an effective basis for partnership between Vichy France and Germany. He was to be speedily disillusioned. Hitler had no intention of treating Vichy France as an equal partner, and a meeting between Pétain and Hitler at Montoire in December 1940 achieved absolutely nothing. Despite Pétain's boast that he had been able to alleviate the armistice conditions, 1.9 million French soldiers were held in captivity, giving the Germans their strongest bargaining counter with the Vichy regime. Hitler, in any case, showed his contempt for Vichy illusions about equality days later by deporting 70,000 Lorrainers into the Unoccupied Zone without consultation.

Marshall Pétain and Pierre Laval at Vichy, November 1942

The characteristics of the Vichy regime soon began to emerge on the home front. First of all, it was profoundly conservative and anti-democratic. An early law removed a prohibition on racist comments in the press, and great national newspapers like *Le Temps* (Time) became little more than government propaganda sheets. Laval's 'Radio Lyon' was another instrument of Vichy propaganda. Trade unions were soon dissolved and replaced by professional corporations which were supposed to represent the workers, the employers and the government. As in Mussolini's Italy, the power of such corporations was heavily weighted in favour of the employers and the government. Workers were expected to know their place in Vichy France and to obey *les patrons*. The peasants showed the 'right' spirit by acclaiming Pétain as 'the Peasant Marshal', the spiritual head of their peasant class. There was to be no questioning of authority under Le Maréchal. Children chanted slogans like *'Maréchal, nous voila'* (Marshal, we are here).

There was a nod in the direction of social reform with old age pensions, and state-funded physical exercise for the young. But divorce was made more difficult, reflecting the regime's alliance with the Catholic Church with its emphasis on family life. Surprisingly, perhaps, Vichy resisted the Church's attempt to reclaim control of education.

Vichy's claim to be bringing about a 'national revolution' was at best a half truth. It was a conservative revolution which destroyed the Republic of the parties with, it must be admitted, the help of those parties, but Vichy's gaze was fixed firmly on the past. A past, French people were told, with the timeless values of a Catholic peasant France.

Nevertheless the 'national revolution' did receive the support of the broad mass of French men and women. How do we account for this? Clearly the trauma of 1940 had something to do with it. Everyone in France, bar de Gaulle's tiny minority, expected Germany to win the war (in a famous phrase, General Weygand said 'in three weeks Great Britain will have its neck wrung like a chicken'). Many, especially on the political Right, did blame the chaotic politics of the Third Republic for France's defeat. The defeat of 1940 offered these forces a change of revenge against the leftists of the Popular Front who had threatened middle-class privileges. Above all, in the towering, venerable figure of 'the Marshal', France had a reassuring heroic figure from the past, who had foreseen her defeat and could now be trusted to steer her through the dangers presented by a German-dominated Europe. Some even fooled themselves into believing that somehow the Marshal was playing a 'double game' and was biding his time, waiting for a chance to reassert French power against Germany. There is little evidence to support such an interpretation.

Lastly, in 1940 there was a strongly anti-British feeling in the country, obviously strengthened by what had happened at Mers-el-Kébir. The British (as usual) had let France down, and the best that the majority of French people could do seemingly was to settle down and accommodate themselves with Hitler's 'New Order'. In most instances, this meant not active collaboration but acceptance of France's defeat and occupation. It is, of course, still possible to criticise the majority of the French population for not resisting the Occupation more actively despite the trauma of 1940, but, given the ruthlessness of the Nazi occupiers, is it fair to do so?

The second major characteristic of the Vichy regime was its racism, and Pétain himself was anti-Semitic. Evidence of this anti-Semitism emerged within three months of the establishment of Vichy, when Pétain promulgated the Statuits des Juifs (the Jewish Statutes). Under their provisions anyone with three Jewish grandparents was defined as Jewish, or two grandparents if his or her spouse was Jewish. Jews were excluded from the officer corps, the judiciary, teaching, all elected offices and the press. The assets of important Jewish families such as the Rothschilds were seized. All this encouraged the general harassment of Jews in France and brought shame on her name, especially in 1942 when French police helped round up Jews for deportation to German death camps. This anti-Semitic campaign was made more nauseating by the fact that Jews with honourable war records were protected from persecution by Marshal Pétain. However, even this protection did not last. Jews could fight and die for France, but they were not to be accepted as full citizens. An earlier decree in July 1940 had already stripped thousands of them of their French citizenship.

In other respects, Vichy followed policies which reflected the difficulties which would have faced any French government in June 1940. The armistice had left 65 per cent of France's industry and 60 per cent of her cultivated land in German hands. The cost of the German occupation had to be paid for by the French, and the chaos surrounding the battle in 1940 had disrupted the harvest. Vichy also had to introduce rationing in the winter of 1940-1.

A last feature of the so-called 'national revolution' was a desire for revenge. In the minds of the Vichyites the defeat of 1940 was a result of the sins of the Third Republic, and its leaders had to be punished. Daladier and Blum were imprisoned, and in 1942 they were brought to trial at Riom. In the event, the trial was so embarrassing for Pétain and his associates when charges could not be made to stick, that it was quietly dropped. A further vengeful spasm in the hour of defeat resulted in the abolition of local councils, in all communes over 2,000 people. Pétain was no democrat.

5 Laval and Collaboration

Despite the dominance of the Marshal, there was a second distinctive viewpoint in the Vichy leadership. Pétain had naively thought that an anti-communist, traditionalist France could be an equal partner with Germany, but the second central personality at Vichy, Pierre Laval, accepted German dominance and tried to make an accommodation with it. Laval was Pétain's first Prime Minister, but the two men had little in common. Laval was a pacifist who had played a prominent role in French appeasement policy before 1939. He was also a wealthy man of peasant origin, whose swarthy appearance and capacity for intrigue aroused suspicion.

Relations with the Marshal were always uneasy. Laval called Pétain 'a windbag' and the Marshal, somewhat unreasonably, blamed Laval for the failure of the Montoire meeting with Hitler. Pétain used this as an excuse to sack Laval in December 1940. One of the few achievements of this early phase of Lavalism was to secure the return to Paris of the body of Napoleon I's son, the Duc de Reichstadt. There is evidence of a plot organised by Laval to lure Pétain to Paris for the ceremony, after which he would not be allowed to return to the Unoccupied Zone. Pétain would not go, however, and Laval was sacked instead.

For a time Laval was forced to cultivate his links with the collaborationists in Paris, who were even more pro-German than the Vichyites. Meanwhile Admiral Darlan, the head of the French navy, replaced Laval as Vichy Prime Minister. Darlan believed, like Laval, in co-operation with the Germans, but he was primarily concerned with Vichy's relationship with the French colonies.

The Germans wanted facilities in French North Africa and Syria and the May Protocols in 1942 conceded these to them, but Darlan's policy merely provoked the British. They organised an attack on Syria with de Gaulle's Free French forces, and the Vichy garrison was expelled. Other Vichy leaders then became alarmed about the extent of Darlan's collaboration with the Germans. They persuaded Pétain to remove him in April 1942 (although he remained Commander-in-Chief of the navy) and to bring back Laval as Prime Minister. This was done because the Germans saw Laval as their best ally, and persuaded a reluctant Pétain to reinstate him.

Laval's return to the premiership came about in quite different European circumstances. In June 1941 Hitler had attacked the USSR, and Laval was an enthusiastic anti-Communist. Motivated by a mixture of pacifism and pragmatism, he hailed Nazi Germany as the saviour of Europe from Bolshevism. He then threw in his lot with Germany, despite the growing evidence in 1942 that Hitler might not win the war. In November the Anglo-Americans invaded French North Africa and Darlan switched sides. The Germans retaliated by trying to seize the great French fleet in Toulon harbour after invading and occupying the area under Vichy rule. However, in a last and somewhat uncharacteristic defiant gesture, Darlan had arranged for the French warships to be scuttled. He himself was the victim of an obscure assassination plot some weeks later.

France was now totally under German occupation, and this increased Laval's influence because he was Germany's man. However, it was in a context of increasing German repression and growing popular resistance. Deportations of French workers to Germany increased, and there was nothing Pétain or Laval could do about it, other than issue mild protests. This had the major effect of making thousands of French men and women flee to join the French Resistance.

6 De Gaulle and the Resistance

To begin with, as we have seen, General de Gaulle had minimal support both inside and outside France. He was tolerated by Churchill, the British Prime Minister, but Vichy sentenced him to death in his absence. De Gaulle was anxious to show that the Free French Movement was effective, but an expedition against Dakar in French Senegal in 1940 was an embarrassing fiasco. When the Americans came into the war in 1941 they preferred General Giraud as leader of the Free French and President Roosevelt actively disliked de Gaulle. Only as the involvement of Free French forces in the war grew, did de Gaulle begin to increase in stature, although the Americans continued to distrust him. The Free French (La France Combattante) forces in North Africa, for example, played a distinguished role in the battles against the German Afrika Korps, especially in the heroic defence of Bir-Hakeim. General de Gaulle also had the priceless advantage of becoming well known to the French people via his BBC radio broadcasts, and Giraud was too lacking in leadership qualities to outmanoeuvre his rival in the battle for the leadership of the Free French Movement.

a) The Resistance

Inside France Resistance developed slowly after 1940, although there were a minority of resisters from the beginning of the German occupation. The Germans (under orders from Hitler) were on their best behaviour at the outset of the occupation, but small resistance groupings appeared first of all in the occupied zone where the German forces were obviously visible. But so was the Gestapo (German Secret Police) which ruthlessly eliminated these groups in 1941.

In the unoccupied zone, matters were more complex. Resisters had to make a choice of resisting not the German enemy, but a regime operated by fellow countrymen which had the support of the majority of French people. It, too, had its police apparatus, the notorious *milice*, which was as bad, if not worse than the Gestapo. Nevertheless, it was in the unoccupied zone that the most significant resistance groupings emerged. Combat (largely Catholic) had a mainly middle-class membership of engineers, teachers and former army officers, while Libération was the movement of the socialists and the trades unionists.

The most controversial segment of the resistance movement was the

PCF. Between 1939 and 1941, the French Communists, in name at least, were allies of the Nazis, however repugnant this situation was to individual party members (a result of the Nazi-Soviet Pact of 1939). After June 1941 when Hitler invaded the USSR the Communists were wholehearted enemies of the Germans and the single most potent grouping in the entire resistance movement. In 1945 they were to claim that 75,000 party members died in the struggle against the Germans, but effective fighters though they were, the Communists weakened the overall resistance between 1941 and 1943. This was because they refused to co-operate with other non-Communist resisters and were often openly hostile to them. The PCF had its own agenda to set up a worker's state in France and other groups like Combat were regarded as bourgeois reactionaries. It was a great triumph, therefore, for de Gaulle and the Free French when his agent Jean Moulin (parachuted into France by the British) persuaded the PCF to join the Council for National Resistance in 1943, accept de Gaulle's leadership and work with the non-Communist groups. Six weeks after this triumph, Moulin was captured by the Gestapo and tortured to death, a signal example of the price resisters often paid.

The formation of the CNR prepared the way for the Resistance's greatest triumphs, when it disrupted crucial parts of the German communication system at the time of the Anglo-American invasion in June 1944. Railway lines were blown up and bridges destroyed, which meant that important German reinforcements failed to reach the front line in time. In the south especially, pitched battles were fought with the Germans in the scrubland or *maquis,* which gave the Resistance a new name.

Despite its considerable achievements, it has to be admitted that the Resistance was joined by as few as 2 per cent of the French population. What does this suggest about its overall significance? Clearly most of the French population were not disposed to join, and some regarded it as a dangerous nuisance which brought down German reprisals upon them (it was commonplace for dozens of French hostages to be shot after some act of resistance). Neither could the Resistance claim (as, for example, in Yugoslavia) to have liberated the country. This was the achievement of the Anglo-American armies, even if some Free French units fought alongside them.

Any answer to this question must be speculative. The Resistance certainly provided post-war France with a generation of political leaders from de Gaulle to Mitterrand. It also provided the country with a reminder that not all French men and women accepted defeat and collaboration with fascism. Whether, as historians have suggested, the Resistance restored French honour after 1940 and Vichy's collaborationism, must remain a matter for debate. Most of the French people were not resisters, and France alone of the occupied countries of Western Europe had a legitimate government which chose to collaborate with the Nazis. Conversely, it took great courage to resist such a ruthless authoritarian tyranny as Nazi Germany and its Vichy surrogate, and individuals with such courage can be hard to find.

It can also be argued that the blood sacrifice of the Resistance gave France a place at the conference table for the post-war settlement, which in terms of her overall contribution to the war, she was hardly entitled to. The crusty, unyielding personality of the Free French leader, Charles de Gaulle, ensured that France would be treated like a great power, but arguably it was men like Jean Moulin who gave her claim to that status some legitimacy.

7 The End of Vichy

Pétain's 'National Revolution' became defunct when the Germans invaded the Unoccupied Zone in November 1942. But the Germans clung to their creatures, and a puppet government led by Pétain made a pathetic plea to de Gaulle for co-operation before this.

The Allied victory in 1945 sealed the fate of the two Vichy leaders and they were both brought to trial after the war. Pétain, although he claimed (possibly falsely) that old age had weakened his faculties, was nevertheless sentenced to death. However, de Gaulle commuted the sentence to life imprisonment. The Marshal died in 1951. Laval was not so lucky. His trial was a charade, as some of his prosecutors had Vichy associations themselves, and he was sentenced to death by firing squad. In reality, Laval was the scapegoat for the guilt of many French people who preferred to obliterate the wartime years from memory.

Vichy continued to have its defenders, however. Some French historians argued that the Collaboration d'État (State Collaboration) of the Vichy government under Pétain and Laval protected the French people from even more repressive German behaviour. Others have pointed out that the Vichy regime conspicuously failed to prevent the deportation of many thousands of French people to Germany as slave labourers, or the milking of the French economy by the occupiers. Any judgement of Vichy, therefore, depends on whether it is concluded that its supporters were genuine French patriots who recognised the apparent hopelessness of France's position, or whether they are adjudged to have been fascist sympathisers who took advantage of France's catastrophic defeat in 1940.

Was Pétain a fascist? His regime certainly had many of the characteristics of fascism (in its authoritarianism and anti-Semitism), and he and Laval seemed convinced that Germany would win the war. But other leading Vichy figures were *attentiste* (wait and see) who were not naturally pro-German or pro-fascist. They accepted the reality of German domination in 1940 but were prepared to change sides later. A third group in Occupied France, which remained distinct from the Vichyites, were the French Nazis who were genuine supporters of

Hitlerism. So the collaborationist movement after 1940 had different layers to it, but all are open to the accusation that they betrayed France's national interest. State collaboration, 'wait and see' and outright fascism alike rejected the possibility of resistance envisaged by General de Gaulle. Alone of the occupied Western European states, France did not have a government in exile in 1940. Realism or treachery? The debate about Vichy France goes on.

8 *L'épuration* (The Purging)

Before France could settle to any degree of post-war normalcy there had to be a reckoning. This was the settling of scores in 1944 with those who had betrayed the Republic by serving Vichy and by collaborating with the Germans. This process is known as *L'épuration*. It was a bloody affair, symbolised by newsreels showing French women having their heads shaved for going out with Germans and crowds physically attacking and abusing alleged Vichyites.

Like almost everything else in France associated with the war and the occupation, *l'épuration* has given rise to profound controversy and bitterness. Was there, as the Vichyites later claimed, an orgy of destruction and peremptory justice in the period before de Gaulle's authority became effective? Or was there just a thoroughgoing expulsion of the Vichyites from the corridors of power which they had haunted, to France's shame, since 1940?

The evidence is ambivalent. The historian Robert Aron later estimated that there were between 30,000 and 40,000 summary executions (that is executions carried out without the sanction of any central political authority) before September 1944. But the Comité d'Histoire de la Deuxième Guerre Mondiale (Historical Committee on the Second World War) produced much lower figures of 9,000 summary executions after the Allied landings in Normandy in June 1944, followed by over 700 executions afterwards by due legal process. Post-war hatreds between Left and Right also befogged the issue, for with the coming of the Cold War tales about 'Communist Justice' in the immediate Liberation period (allegedly designed to wipe out leading anti-Communists) became popular on the French Right. It is unlikely that the exact truth will ever be known but the measured judgement of one historian that *l'épuration* was too often about settling old political scores seems fair.

That a 'self-healing' process had not taken place in 1944 was to be made only too clear in the post-war decades when accusations were made about the wartime activities of numerous public figures, with ex-Resistance members still intent on exacting revenge on those who had (allegedly) collaborated with Vichy and the Germans. In the 1970s a notable French film called *The Sorrow and the Pity* re-awoke the controversy, and even in the 1990s the case of Paul Touvier (hidden by

Catholic clerics after accusations that he had been responsible for the murder of Jews) caused bitter dispute.

One historian has also pointed out that the scale of 'the purging' was very limited. As late as 1958, following a political amnesty declared in 1953, there were still 14 ex-Vichyites sitting in the French Parliament. Many others survived in the diplomatic service, the judiciary and among the local government *prefecture* (prefects). This reflected a whole society's embarrassment about confronting the issue of Vichyism.

The Fall of France	**Occupation and Resistance**
The *drôle de guerre* and its significance	De Gaulle and Pétain
Battle of France. French defeat. How and why	The characteristics of Vichy
The armistice and its effects	Internal and external resistance. Liberation

Summary - 'The Fall of France and the Vichy Regime'

Making notes on *'The Fall of France and the Vichy Regime'*

There are two distinct elements in this chapter. One deals with France's catastrophic military defeat in 1940, the other with the German occupation and those who resisted it or collaborated with it. The headings and sub-headings given below can be used when compiling a basic set of factual notes on these two topics. It is also important that you make clear notes about the historical controversy over the reasons why France fell in 1940. You should be consciously aware that the chapter presents a revisionist view on this issue which contradicts the more traditional one.

1   The *drôle de guerre*
1.1 France's passive reaction to the coming of war.
1.2 The Army and the 'joke war'.
1.3 The 'sideshows'.
2   The Battle of France
2.1 French pre-war planning.
2.2 The German offensive.
2.3 The Government reshuffle.

Answering essay questions on *'The Fall of France and the Vichy Regime'*

Essay questions on this topic tend to focus on either the fall of France or on occupation and resistance. As traditional explanations of the fall of France place emphasis on a number of factors that pre-date the war, you would be expected to bring these into an essay answer. Make a conscious effort to identify these factors. This might involve looking at the the notes you made on Chapters 2 and 3. Study the following questions:

1   'France's defeat in 1940 was more political than military.' Discuss.
2   Examine the view that the French defeat in 1940 was more to do with French deficiencies than German brilliance.
3   In what sense, if any, could the Vichy regime be described as fascist?
4   Compare and contrast the roles of Pétain and de Gaulle between 1940 and 1944.
5   Why did so few French people support the Resistance between 1940 and 1944?

A useful exercise would be to think about which of the essays would be the most difficult to answer and why. Many would feel that Question 4 would be the most difficult because it asks you not only to compare the roles of the individuals mentioned but also requires you to contrast them as well - in other words, find not just points of similarity but points of difference, too.

Essay questions invariably have a 'hidden agenda'. Question 1, for example, focuses on military and political factors, but it is important that economic factors are also discussed. The fact that a question focuses on one particular aspect does not mean that other aspects can be ignored. Make sure, too, that when, as in Question 1, you are asked to 'discuss', you do just that. Another key word that frequently occurs - as in Questions 1 and 2 - is 'more'. This normally requires you to make some sort of judgement about which is the more important of the factors mentioned. Again, in Question 3 note the key words, 'if any'. You may feel that Vichy was not fascist. If this is the case you will need to produce plenty of evidence to back up your argument.

Above all, avoid the 'narrative trap' - just writing down the facts without really answering the question. All the questions demand thought and good answers are always characterised by a real effort to answer the question. Hence the importance of planning your essay. Relevance is vital.

Source-based questions on *'The Fall of France and the Vichy Regime'*

1 The Phoney War
Carefully study the photograph on page 83. Answer the following questions:
a) What does the photograph tell us about the attitude of the soldiers? (2 marks)
b) In what sense does the source contribute to the more traditional explanation for France's defeat in 1940? (5 marks)
c) Can you suggest a link between the *drôle de guerre* and the condition of the soldiers? (3 marks)

CHAPTER 6

The Fourth Republic, 1946–58

1 Constitutional Development

The first problem facing post-war France was constitution making. General de Gaulle succeeded in absorbing the leaders of the Resistance movement, including the French Communist party (PCF), into a provisional government of national union with he himself as acting head of government. At the same time, he was able to persuade the semi-independent former Resistance Committees to hand over local administration to centrally appointed prefects, thus restoring France's traditional highly centralised system of government. These processes were complete by the end of 1944.

Before the central government in Paris had properly imposed its authority on the country, however, France experienced the period in 1944-5 known as *l'épuration* or the purging during which unofficial and often bloody justice was meted out to former Vichy collaborators. An official legal process was then set up by the Provisional Government to deal with those who were deemed to have betrayed their country. However, De Gaulle's priority was not revenge on Vichy but the securing of a strong American-style presidency which would dominate a weak legislature. He hoped that this would be a means of avoiding the political weakness of the Third Republic with its strong but chronically divided legislature and weak and almost decorative presidency. To this end he arranged for a referendum to be held in October 1945. This put a formal end to the Third Republic because the majority voted in favour of there being a new constitution. On the same day a Constituent Assembly (Parliament) was also elected, with the task of drawing up a constitution for the new Fourth Republic.

Things did not go smoothly. De Gaulle resigned in January 1946 (disgusted by party feuding in the new Parliament) before a referendum approving the new constitution could be held. When it was, in May 1946, the electorate surprisingly rejected the plan for a new uni-cameral or one-chamber system by a majority of over a million. One possible explanation for this setback is the widespread fear that the Communists, at the time the largest party in the Constituent Assembly, might dominate in a system where there was no upper house to balance the power of the Assembly. A second referendum in 1946 then approved a constitution for the Fourth Republic which was virtually indistinguishable from that of the Third Republic. France had not secured the strong executive presidency which de Gaulle had craved.

The new legislature consisted of two chambers, the National Assembly and the Council of the Republic. The President as Head of State was to be elected by both Chambers for seven-year terms. He was to appoint as Prime Minister a member of the National Assembly who could secure a majority there. The Deputies in the National Assembly were to be elected by a system of proportional representation, while the Council of the Republic was to be nominated by the government. Real power, as was the case under the Third Republic, would lie with the Chamber.

In de Gaulle's absence after 1946 French politics were dominated by what was known as 'tripartism', whereby governments were dominated by a loose alliance of the Socialists, the Communists, and the centre-right MRP (Mouvement Républicain Populaire or Popular Republican Movement). Tripartism broke down in 1947 when the Communists left the government, and the Fourth Republic suffered another blow when the right-wing Gaullist RPF (Rassemblement du Peuple Français or Rally of the French People) was set up in 1947. Both the RPF and the Communists proceeded to attack the Fourth Republic and 'the system'. Thus, a major theme of the Fourth Republic's history emerged before 1951, whereby the far Right and far Left excluded themselves from the political mainstream, and governments could only be formed from the centre-right and centre-left, the so-called 'Third Force'. Weak and palsied government by coalition was a consequence (as no single party could claim the support of even a third of the electorate), with the exception of the period in 1954-5 when Mendés-France made a vigorous attempt to introduce a reform programme.

A second and contradictory theme of the period 1944 to 1958 concerns the economy. For despite its apparent political weakness, the Fourth Republic made a vigorous economic recovery from the war and maintained this recovery into the 1950s. Here American economic aid and effective central planning were crucial factors. Associated with them was France's membership, from 1951 onwards, of supranational economic bodies such as the ECSC (European Coal and Steel Community) and the EEC (European Economic Community), which gave her access to a wider Western European market.

A third major theme of the period was France's difficult colonial heritage in Indo-China and Algeria. Colonial wars in both areas divided French society and resulted, in Indo-China, in humiliating defeat and withdrawal in 1954. Algeria, which broke into bloody insurrection in the same year, was to precipitate a military and political crisis which both brought de Gaulle back to power in 1958 and destroyed the Fourth Republic.

2 De Gaulle and the Parties

De Gaulle never hid his opinion of the political parties. Writing later in his memoirs he was to say:

> As I saw it, the State must have a head, that is a leader whom the nation could see beyond its own fluctuations, a man in charge of

essential matters and the guarantor of its fate. It was also necessary that this executive must not originate in Parliament.

The key phrase here was 'must not originate in Parliament' for de Gaulle remained profoundly suspicious of the old political parties which he blamed for the defeat of 1940. As Head of State in 1945, he had found the wranglings of party politicians distasteful and had even found the task of sitting on the government front bench in the Constituent Assembly irksome. Yet what alternative did de Gaulle have to offer? He was always offended by opponents' accusations of 'Bonapartism' (that is trying to set up a military dictatorship like Napoleon Bonaparte's), but remained convinced that in some way the party politicians could not adequately represent the French national interest. This ambivalence about the nature of democracy underlaid all the disputes de Gaulle had with the old parties of the Third Republic between 1944 and his resignation in January 1946.

Critics suggested that as a military man de Gaulle lacked that ability to compromise which is essential in a democratic politicians, and there were many stories about his authoritarianism in this early post-war period. One colleague reported that in Cabinet it was forbidden to smoke unless the General did so first, to question him, or even to take notes! In fact, the accusation about inflexibility was shown to be unfounded by what happened when de Gaulle returned to power in 1958. Nevertheless, as one historian has pointed out, in 1946 he seemed to lack the mollifying skills he showed after 1958, when he manipulated party politicians with rare skill. Why was de Gaulle unable to work with the politicians when elements in at least one of the major political parties, the Mouvement Républicain Populaire (MRP), were very much in sympathy with the General, and when the other two major old-style parties, the Communists and the Socialists, were initially well disposed towards him?

De Gaulle should have been assisted by the Socialists' suspicion of their Communist allies (an inheritance from the pre-war period) whom they feared were planning to swallow them up. But his autocratic behaviour alienated the Socialist leader Léon Blum, despite the fact that both men had distinguished anti-fascist records.

Despite the Socialist support in 1945 for de Gaulle's exclusion of the Communists from key ministries (like defence), they joined with them in opposing his plan for a strong executive presidency. He was both offended when Blum refused a post in his government, and angered when the Socialists threatened to leave his government in June 1945. Surprisingly, given de Gaulle's known anti-Communism, relations with the PCF were initially quite cordial and when the Communist leader Thorez returned to France from wartime exile in Moscow, he agreed to disband the Communist militias and to serve in the Provisional Government. Thorez then saw France (as apart from Britain or the

USA) as an ally of the USSR, and agreed with de Gaulle on the paramount need for national unity and the restoration of the French economy. For his part, de Gaulle was relieved that Thorez had taken over control of the PCF rather than other Communist leaders who had been involved in the Resistance and who might have challenged his authority. But the Communists, too, threatened to leave the government in June 1945 because of disagreements about colonial policy (see page 107).

The MRP was the only party to emerge directly from the wartime experience and it contained many former Resistance members. In essence it was part of that Christian Democratic and largely Catholic movement which was to play a vital role in the politics of the whole of post-war Western Europe, and as such was apparently very much in tune with de Gaulle's own profoundly patriotic and Catholic spirit. Again, however, personal antipathy, this time for the MRP leader Georges Bidault (who in turn could not stand the General) combined with ideological division, to make co-operation difficult. De Gaulle objected to the MRP's support for alignment with the Socialists in a centre-left coalition, and to its general sympathy for nationalising policies. This was part of a general shift to the Left in French politics after 1944, so that the old Radical party declined to only about 10 per cent in national support, and the Right to 16 per cent.

Paradoxically, while de Gaulle seems to have recognised this leftward shift, he still reserved for himself a special role as a national saviour who was above all parties. He told a member of the MRP that 'the Right is outside the Nation, while the Left is outside the State', a characteristi- cally mystical statement that showed his conviction that somehow cross-party consensus could be created by him where none existed. The role of 'de Gaulle' (his memoirs always referred to himself rather grandly in the third person!) was to create such a consensus, and he became irritated when individuals like Blum or Bidault showed greater loyalty to their political parties than to his perception of the national interest. The same MRP members commented on de Gaulle's essential contempt for all political parties.

3 De Gaulle's Retirement

It is clear that from October 1945 onwards, de Gaulle became increasingly disenchanted with a situation in which the Assembly was dominated by three parties of roughly equal size which refused to give him the executive powers he assumed should be his. Yet he did not help his cause by obdurately refusing to associate himself with any one party, which would have allowed him to campaign for his demands.

Nevertheless, there has been considerable controversy among historians about the motives behind the resignation. The classic explanation, put forward by Pierre Goubert and James MacMillan, has been that de Gaulle saw his resignation merely as a tactical device before *l'appel* (the call) would come again from desperate politicians who would be quite unable to run the country without him. He did not expect to wait long. This conflicts rather with the accounts given by de Gaulle himself at the time:

> 1 I consider that my mission is ended. France is free: she took part in the final victory. France is on the Rhine, her Empire is free and defended; we are going back to Indo-China. At home there are regular elections, so democracy has been re-established; I
> 5 considered that my role was over on 21 October 1945. I already wanted to go then, but since there was unanimity behind my name in the Constituent Assembly, I stayed. The three parties continue to attack one another and are preoccupied with the forthcoming elections - it is my view that this is a misfortune for France - and I
> 10 have no intention of taking part in these party struggles.

This account of what de Gaulle said to Cabinet colleagues at the time, given by the then Socialist Minister of Agriculture, also conflicts with what he said to his nephew some years later when he confessed:

> I have made at least one political mistake in my life: my departure in January 1946. I thought the French would recall me very quickly. Because they didn't do so, France wasted several years.

This statement, with its characteristically egotistical ring, has the smack of truth about it, although de Gaulle's recent biographer has a more mundane alternative explanation of the circumstances surrounding his resignation. Jean Lacouture suggests that the retirement was part of a longer-term plan for de Gaulle's life after six years of extreme effort. This involved rebuilding his house at Colombey-les-Deux-Eglises which had been wrecked by the Germans during the Occupation, seeing his daughter married (another who was retarded had died young), and writing his memoirs. Nonetheless, Lacouture concedes that de Gaulle was convinced that, sooner or later, 'the call' would come.

Could de Gaulle, with all his suspicions of party politicians, have created a workable new constitution in 1945-6? Frank Giles argues that had the General been more tactful, instead of scornful and hostile, in his dealings with the parliamentary parties, the story might have been different in 1946, but that his inability to compromise would probably have made collision inevitable.

These rival interpretations are important because Gaullist legend insists that de Gaulle was merely fulfilling his destiny in retiring from the scene to await a more opportune historic moment. Historians sympathetic to de Gaulle have tended to go along with the General's own estimate of himself as a man of destiny, called to save France from disaster. The less sympathetic regard the resignation of January 1946 as an example of his overweening ambition, and intolerance, which made it impossible for him to work in a truly parliamentary system. We are left with a paradox, a man who was revolted by dictatorship yet loathed the cut and thrust of parliamentary politics. Which was the real de Gaulle?

4 Economic Recovery

In some respects, the French economy was in a worse condition in 1944 than it had been at the end of the First World War. This was certainly true in respect of damage to property, for two million buildings had been destroyed in France in the course of the Second World War. Inflation was rampant and there were severe food shortages in the cities, although the peasantry still managed to eat well through skilful manipulation of the black market in agricultural goods. When the shortage of basic commodities such as coal and the disruption of the communication system by heavy Allied bombing before the 'D Day' invasion are also taken into account, the considerable task facing the Provisional Government becomes clear. The reconstruction needed an innovative and imaginative series of reforms which would radically change the structure and operation of the French economy. This happened when, inside a few months in 1944-5, the coalmines of the North, the Renault car factories, the Bank of France, the aircraft industry, the credit system, and four of the biggest deposit banks were nationalised.

These changes reflected the post-war leftward shift in French politics that has been already remarked upon. But a more significant development in the economic sphere was the conversion of virtually all French politicians to the philosophy of *dirigisme*, or centrally-directed State planning. This included de Gaulle himself who was enthusiastic about the state-controlled economy saying that: 'We want it to be the State which, for the benefit of all, spearheads the economic effort of the entire nation, and acts in such a way as to improve the life of each French man and woman.' How do we account for this transformation in economic thinking on the French Right and Centre in the post-war period? In part, it seems to have been a response to the discrediting of right-wing ideology by the Vichy experience, but also a reflection of a general desire for a more humane and caring society as a result of the suffering and destruction caused by the war.

Given the general acceptance of the need for state-directed planning in post-war France, there remained the need to create instruments to do the job efficiently. At the bureaucratic level, the École Nationale d'Administration (School of National Administration) provided for the training of civil servants, but more important was the Commissariat Général au Plan (General Planning Office). This was staffed by top civil servants and technocrats and directed what became known as the 'Monnet Plan' (after Jean Monnet, its director) which aimed to direct 'the modernisation and equipment of metropolitan and overseas France'. A tinge of Gaullist authoritarianism is suggested by the fact that the decree instigating the Plan was put into operation in January 1946 without Parliament ever being consulted. Nonetheless, it was the Monnet Plan which provided the driving force behind French economic recovery, which culminated in impressive economic growth in the 1950s and 1960s.

However, it is questionable whether 'the Plan' and its *dirigiste* philosophy was the main cause of France's recovery, as some of its keenest admirers have attempted to suggest. Evidence that it was not is provided by the fact that France benefited greatly from American Marshall Aid (named after the then US Secretary of State for Foreign Affairs) to the tune of $2,500 billion between 1948 and 1952. One historian has observed that this US aid kept the momentum of the recovery going at a point when France's own resources would have been overstretched. The technocrats and economists of the Commissariat Général du Plan then ensured that the aid was used effectively to stimulate and maintain economic growth.

5 A Gaullist Comeback?

It was always de Gaulle's intention to return to politics and he was surrounded by sympathisers whose main aim was to propel him back into the political limelight. De Gaulle took little persuading, particularly as he thoroughly disapproved of the eventual shape which the constitution of the Fourth Republic took. He had welcomed the first rejection of the constitution, and in a speech at Bayeux in June 1946 he again put forward his own proposals for a strong executive presidency. This brought a rebuke from the veteran socialist Léon Blum who accused the General of being 'swamped by elements of a totalitarian mentality' and 'a prisoner of his illusions'.

Blum's rebuke had no effect because de Gaulle announced the existence of a new movement, the RPF (Rassemblement du Peuple Français or Rally of the French People) in a speech in April 1947:

> It is time for the Rassemblement of the French People to be formed and organized, so that, within the framework of the law, over and above differences of opinion, the great effort of common salvation and the profound reform of the State may be begun and triumph.

The theme was the same. France needed salvation and de Gaulle was to be her saviour, a concept which historians have called democratic paternalism. But confusingly, although de Gaulle said that the RPF was a movement of the French people and not a political party, he allowed it to take part in parliamentary elections. Why did de Gaulle choose this particular moment to try to relaunch his political career? One factor seems to have been the onset of the Cold War in 1947 with the fear of Soviet expansion (see page 107) which allowed the General to convince himself that 'Of course, there'll be a war'. Another was that in the summer of 1947 the PCF had been excluded from the government, now led by a Socialist Prime Minister, and had called for a strike against the government by its sister trade union organisation, the CGT. There was also a deteriorating situation in French Indo-China (see page 107) which alarmed the government and which produced a confused response. One of De Gaulle's recent biographers notes that in this stormy and difficult situation the General was sure that his stature as a leader would be recognised.

However, there was still confusion about exactly what the RPF's political role was supposed to be. When questioned about it, de Gaulle replied: 'Experience, yesterday and today, has shown that the single party is nothing more than a dictatorship. We shall not be returning to such follies, which are contrary to our ideal.' The press accused de Gaulle of 'Bonapartism' and the general public appeared to be equally confused, as an opinion poll in late May 1949 gave the RPF an approval rating of only 26 per cent (the same as the Communists). Nevertheless, the stance taken by the RPF on the General's instructions meant that it, like the PCF, was opposed to the Fourth Republic. De Gaulle's populism alarmed the Socialists so that they created a so-called 'Third Force' which, by allying them with the Radicals and other parties, re-created the sort of centre-left coalition so typical of pre-war years.

Until 1951 the RPF, despite de Gaulle's ambivalence about parliamentary politics, continued to poll well in elections but thereafter defections weakened it and by the mid-50s, to the General's disgust, it was indistinguishable from other political parties.

What in the end was the RPF? On the one hand, it did take part in parliamentary elections as a political party, for example, winning 107 seats in the 1951 elections. On the other hand, it claimed to be 'the rally' of the entire French nation (underlining the point previously made about de Gaulle's conviction that neither the Right nor the Left could truly represent the nation). MacMillan notes that the RPF had 'parallels with fascist movements', and Lacouture concludes that although it was intended to be a reformist movement, the RPF soon became obsessed with fighting communism.

Certainly anti-communism was a popular cause in the period 1947-51, and de Gaulle made craftily coded attacks on the PCF in his speeches in which he referred to the Communists, not directly, as 'separatists' (because their first loyalty was to Moscow and not to France). But the doubts remain about whether de Gaulle was ever, in the truest sense, a democrat. This is particularly so as once the RPF began to behave like any other political party, he disavowed it, and retired once again into sulky political exile.

The concrete results of the appearance of the RPF were two. It marked the end of 'tripartism' whereby the PCF, the MRP and the Socialists had run the country in uneasy alliance since the elections of October 1945. It also dealt a severe blow to the electoral appeal of the MRP which had claimed to be 'the party of fidelity' (i.e. loyal to de Gaulle) and which in its weakened shape became part of that 'Third Force' which was formed to resist the challenge from the PCF and the RPF. There was a considerable irony in the fact that, although the RPF became strongly anti-Communist, it, like the Communists, was regarded as a threat to the existence of the Fourth Republic in the years before 1951.

6 The Exclusion of the Communists

Between 1945 and 1947 the French Communists were part of the French government. Between 1947 and 1981 no Communist held a ministerial position. This was one of the central features of French post-war politics, as it had been in the inter-war period when the Communists had been in power just once - in 1936.

Throughout the period after the Second World War (at least until the 1980s) the PCF retained a good deal of popular support. However, suspicion of it was strengthened by the coming of the Cold War after which European Communist parties were seen as surrogates of the USSR. Indeed evidence released after 1947 suggested that while in office the French Communist Party had used its influence to infiltrate Communists on to boards of management in the aircraft industry, and to secure jobs for Communist party members. This created fear in the non-Communist parties that such behaviour was all part of a wider plot, directed from Moscow, to seize power in France. Communist rhetoric with its constant references to revolution merely strengthened this impression.

The exclusion of the Communists from political power, therefore, together with the attitude of the RPF meant that the Fourth Republic had enemies both on the Right and the Left. This narrowed the field from which French governments could be selected, and arguably made it more difficult for them to govern by achieving a working majority in Parliament. Important decisions on foreign policy, colonial policy and economic policy were taken by shaky governments in the knowledge that whatever they did there would be ferocious parliamentary opposition (Algeria and German rearmament were two examples, the second issue uniting the PCF and the RPF).

7 Indo-China

French Indo-China was regarded as the jewel of the empire, and was made up of five regional units. The French-protected kingdoms of Laos and Cambodia, and the kingdom of Vietnam composed of three protectorates (Tonkin in the north, Annam in the centre and Cochin China in the south). In 1945, following the Japanese defeat in the Far East, a complex situation arose whereby in Vietnam, the south was held by the British (pending the return of French rule) and the north, by the Chinese Nationalists, who opposed the return of French rule as did the Americans.

More pertinently, a vibrant Vietnamese nationalist movement known as the Vietminh, which was also Communist, had appeared. This was led by Nguyen Ai Quoc, who became better known as Ho Chi Minh (he who enlightens). He had persuaded the puppet Emperor Bao Dai of Annam (installed by the Japanese), to support a new Democratic Republic of Vietnam. In fact, Bao Dai wrote a warning letter to de Gaulle saying that French influence would remain in Vietnam only 'by frank and open recognition of the independence of Vietnam and by renouncing any idea of re-establishing French authority here under whatever form'.

The French had two options where Indo-China was concerned. They could concede some form of independence which would preserve links with the mother country, or they could adhere rigidly to the pre-war formula and insist on Indo-China's colonial status. Bao Dai had warned about the dangers of the second course and at first the French government did seem prepared to consider some form of autonomy for the various kingdoms of Indo-China. Ho Chi Minh himself was prepared to preserve some links with France, partly because he feared the influence of Vietnam's giant neighbour China. 'It is better,' Ho said, 'to sniff France's dung than eat China's all our lives.' This may not sound very flattering to France, but Ho was a French-educated man who genuinely admired France's culture and traditions.

The French government was divided over the Indo-China issue. The Socialists and Communists were sympathetic to the claims of the Indo-Chinese, but de Gaulle and the centre-right were not. To complicate matters further, the Socialists, who mistrusted the PCF, did not wish to antagonise the centre-right parties in the coalition government by pushing the Indo-China independence issue too far.

In October 1946 Ho Chi Minh visited Paris and seemed prepared to negotiate, but the new French constitution destroyed hopes of agreement by incorporating all the overseas dominions into the French Union (the French version of the Commonwealth), which allowed little prospect of autonomy or eventual independence. He and his colleagues felt betrayed and in December 1946 fighting broke out between the Vietminh and French troops in Indo-China. The French claimed that the Vietminh had attacked them first, but they escalated the conflict by launching a bloody assault on the Vietnamese quarter of the port of Haiphong.

The war which began in 1946 divided French society as well as the

French government. A military fact-finder, General Leclerc, advised that, 'In 1947 France can no longer put down by force a grouping of people which is assuming unity and in which there exists a xenophobic and perhaps a national ideal'. Other military advisers were sure that the Vietminh could be crushed. Public opinion was equally divided. An opinion poll in February 1947 showed that 36 per cent of those questioned supported force, 42 per cent favoured negotiations, and 8 per cent believed that France should leave Indo-China altogether.

As the war dragged on from year to year (it lasted until 1954) it became clear that, although the French could hold the major cities such as Hanoi and Saigon, the Vietminh were dominant in the countryside. It was a classic guerilla struggle in which 150,000 French troops fought a hidden enemy which could always merge itself with the native population. Increasingly, too, domestic opinion in France seemed disinterested in the remote struggle in the Far East. This in turn affected the army's morale, as a French captain told a newspaper:

> We turned in upon ourselves, we lived among ourselves, and we became as touchy and sensitive as men flayed alive. But how great was the despair we felt at being rejected by our country - and how great was our need of fraternity.

The war in Indo-China divided politicians, public opinion, and even the military in France. Why then was it allowed to drag on for eight years? Historians have put forward a variety of explanations. One has been that many politicians and generals in the Fourth Republic, remembering the catastrophic defeat of 1940, were not prepared to contemplate the possibility of another military defeat, least of all at the hands of colonial rebels. Other political leaders, of whom the Socialist Léon Blum was one, believed that order had to be restored in Indo-China before talks with the Vietminh could begin. This meant that Ho Chi Minh and his supporters would have to stop fighting before talks could take place, a formula which the rebels were never likely to accept.

In the wider context of colonialism there were those, largely on the political Right and including (in the early days at least) General de Gaulle, who still saw France as having a civilising mission in the world. They could not believe that the colonised were capable of ruling themselves. Even when, as in Indo-China, there was an educated native élite of colonial administrators, who tended to be of the political Right, they refused to have any dialogue with them. The resolve of such unrepentant imperialists was strengthened in the immediate post-war world by the Cold War context. In the 1940s and early 1950s the Americans believed that there was a worldwide Communist plot to dominate the free world. They encouraged successive French governments to stay in Indo-China, and provided considerable financial assistance to enable them to do so.

However, when all this has been said, the French commitment to Indo-China in a world where de-colonisation was becoming the norm was ultimately half-hearted. The real crisis came in May 1954 when a large garrison under siege in the North Vietnamese outpost of Dien Bien Phu surrendered. French resolve finally cracked. The Americans had refused to provide aerial support, and the French government led by Pierre Mendés-France decided that enough was enough. The Geneva Agreement which followed divided Vietnam into a Communist north and a non-Communist south, with a provision for free elections (which were never in fact held). Laos and Cambodia became independent states also, and French involvement in Indo-China was at an end.

But France's colonial problems were not over, and her setback in Indo-China did not totally convince French politicians that the age of empire had ended. For many of them, not least Charles de Gaulle who had matured in the heyday of the pre-war empire, decolonisation was to be a painful learning process at a time when France was having to reassess her position in both Europe and the world.

8 The 'Third Force'

Between 1946 and 1953 France had eight prime ministers, none of whom were Communists or Gaullists (RPF). In practice they had to be chosen from the so-called 'Third Force' which in the election of 1951 consisted of no less than six parties. Governments during this period were of the centre-right (without the Socialists) or centre-left (with them).

In reality the creation of the Third Force was a result of the growing popular appeal of the RPF. To nullify this the centre parties changed the electoral law (which had been based on proportional representation) before the 1951 election so that the system would favour them and operate against the RPF and the Communists. In the event the changes did not have entirely the expected effect. The RPF still won the largest number of seats (107), although the Communists did get fewer seats with a larger share of the popular vote (25.9 per cent as against 21.7 per cent). But the alliance of centre parties polled more than 50 per cent and took power with 340 seats. As it turned out, the Socialists were to be in opposition from January 1952 to June 1954, so France was ruled exclusively by centre-right coalitions during this time.

The similarity with the inter-war period is clear. Again the Left was excluded from power, as was the far Right (although the RPF could not be described as fascist), and the Fourth Republic like its predecessor was open to the accusation of 'cronyism', a new version of 'the Republic of pals'. This accusation has been firmly refuted by some historians who argue that such a view, while superficially attractive, ignores the very real ideological differences between Right and Left during this period which made the formation of strong governments almost impossible. An additional complication was caused by the revival of the religious issue in the 1950s when the MRP supported State subsidies for Catholic schools, a policy predictably opposed by the Socialists and the Radicals.

9 Mendésisme

Pierre Mendés-France, a member of the Radical Party, was Prime Minister for seven months in 1954-5 - actually the longest term served by any prime minister of the Fourth Republic. As a Radical he was clearly within the political grouping which made up the Third Force, but both at the time and subsequently claims were made that what became known as 'Mendésisme' represented something distinctively new in French politics.

Some things about Mendés certainly were new. He was not, for example, tainted by ministerial office under the Fourth Republic, although he had been a member of de Gaulle's provisional government in 1944-5. He was also Jewish which made him the victim of racist slurs from the Right. But what seemed most distinctive about Mendés was his 'hands on' approach to politics. He wanted to solve problems rather than just keep himself in office like many of his political peers, and to solve problems, Mendés was prepared to appeal directly to the French people in radio broadcasts, a tactic which was not popular with politicians, even those in his own party. Unlike his opponents, too, he had a coherent programme based on his recognition of the need for modernisation, investment and full employment in France. Unusually, Mendés himself had real economic expertise, and was not afraid to argue that industrialisation must take priority over military expenditure and the Indo-China war.

Once in office Mendés unveiled an ambitious economic programme. In August 1954 no less than 120 decrees were promulgated by Parliament. They covered matters as diverse as loans for municipal housing and nuclear research. Mendés was also given special powers over the economy, and in an attempt to improve French competitiveness the government introduced agricultural price supports and cheap loans. Yet, if Mendésisme was 'new,' the French public, as the historian Roger Price has pointed out, showed little interest in the Prime Minister's bold plans to improve the housing and education systems. Much more controversy was aroused by Mendés' campaign against alcoholism (he tried optimistically to get the French to drink more milk) which upset the wine lobby. Ultimately the short life of the Mendés-France government made it impossible to translate such ambitious plans into legislation. On the home front Mendésisme seems to have been more about style than achievement.

Arguably the case for seeing Mendés as an innovative leader is stronger in the sphere of foreign and colonial policy. He ended the Indo China War and conceded independence to Tunisia in 1955. In Europe he tried hard to get the treaty ratifying the European Defence Community (see page 116) through the French Parliament, despite personal reservations about it.

Mendès was young (only 40), charismatic and sure of his long-term goals, but ultimately he achieved little because of the nature of the French political system. He himself noted that 'Parliament legislates and controls the executive but the executive must be in a state to govern ... It must not be stopped in its work by the constant fear of being voted out,' and these remarks, which could just as easily have come from de Gaulle (whom Mendès admired) diagnosed France's political disease accurately enough. The fall of his government in February 1955 provides us with a case study for the fragility of Fourth Republic governments. Mendès-France's ramshackle coalition of Radicals, Socialists and Social Republicans (former RPF) was itself 'voted out' because the PCF disliked it for being capitalist, the MRP suspected it of being 'soft' on Algeria, and the Conservatives feared it was too modernistic. One of Mendès-France's better-known sayings was that 'to govern is to choose' but the experience of his government showed the lack of room for manoeuvre possessed by administrations under the Fourth Republic. The need to keep fragile coalitions together made real policy choices difficult because of the tensions within the coalition.

It may be that, as one historian has argued, the fall of the Mendès government, despite its superficial dynamism, was just another example of the Fourth Republic's 'immobilism' or resistance to change. But Mendès deserves some credit for challenging the alleged inertia of the Fourth Republic from within, instead of just castigating it from the outside like the PCF and RPF, which were never prepared to accept the responsibility of office.

10 Poujadism

The third political 'ism' in France in the 1950s was the curious right-wing phenomenon known as 'Poujadism'. Like Gaullism and unlike Mendésisme, it was a movement characterised by its alienation from the mainstream political system. It took its name from Pierre Poujade, a rumbustious maverick who attacked Mendès-France for being a Jew, was vehemently anti-Communist and a defender of the *petit commerçants* (small shopkeepers) in the economically-depressed south and south-west of France.

Was Poujade a fascist? The French media often thought so, and one newspaper called him 'Poujadolf' because his supporters used rough- house methods to deal with opponents at public meetings. Poujade's ability as a mob orator also reminded people of Hitler and Mussolini. Like them, he represented a class of the economically distressed, in this case of lower middle-class businessmen who were protesting against taxation rates, but unlike them, Poujade proved in the end to have little staying power.

For a while, however, the Poujadists replaced the RPF as the protest party of the Right. Their support reached its zenith in 1956 when their Union et Fraternité (Union and Brotherhood) won 53 seats in the Assembly, and polled two and a half million votes. Afterwards, the movement fell into terminal decline, and the Gaullists regained their position as the populist party of the Right after 1958. Ultimately Poujade's problem was that he had no coherent programme to offer other than a vague protest against alleged central government corruption, and a xenophobic attitude to the Algerian question which opposed any concessions to the Muslims. Whether his movement represented a serious revolutionary threat to the Republic must remain open to doubt.

The political puzzle represented by the Fourth Republic may appear to be a chaotic one. But Gaullism, the Third Force, Mendésisme and Poujadism in their various ways represented the search for an illusory stability in French government and politics. The aims of the various groupings were quite different, Mendés the moderniser had little in common with discontented Poujadist shopkeepers who resented paying their taxes, but there was a common theme of dissatisfaction with the Fourth Republic and its institutions. In the end, the colonial war in Algeria was to create the crisis which allowed one of these forces, Gaullism, to bring down the Fourth Republic in 1958. That does not mean that the downfall of the Fourth Republic was inevitable, however, for it had its successes which are all too easily forgotten.

11 The French Economic Miracle

One of the successes was the economy. France, like West Germany and Italy, had her 'economic miracle' in the 1950s and 1960s. The peak performance actually came at the end of the period under study with the annual growth rate rising to 6.2 per cent between 1968 and 1973, but much of the groundwork had been done in the 1950s when the French steel industry had been modernised and electricity production doubled. A largely agrarian economy was becoming an industrial one, and by 1958 French exports were greater than those of the UK for the first time. Changes in France's infrastructure were also important with heavy investment in the state-owned railway system, the SNCF, which was on its way to becoming one of the most efficient in Europe. In this process of economic expansion, the 'Plan' continued to be of central importance (the Second Plan ran from 1954 to 1958, and the Third from 1958 to 1961). It was a mechanism both for directing investment and encouraging a favourable business climate, and gave the state a leading role in the modernisation of the French economy.

However, the economic miracle brought its own problems. Inflationary pressures were often severe in the 1950s as a result of the increase in the money supply, the abandonment of wartime controls, shortages, and rising wage demands from a workforce determined to protect its living standards. A severe counter-inflationary policy in 1952-3 had some success, but the war in Algeria, the 1956 Suez intervention (which forced up oil prices, see page 117), and the high spending of the Socialist-dominated government on social reforms in the same year, reactivated such pressures thereafter. Yet the effects of inflation were largely counteracted by positive features like rising productivity, and greater mobility in the workforce which saw a transfer of workers from older traditional industries such as agriculture and textiles to newer, more dynamic ones like chemicals, engineering and construction.

A more fundamental issue dominated the economic policy of the Fourth Republic in its latter stages, centred on France's growing involvement in the movement for European integration (this included membership both of the European Coal and Steel Community (1951) and the European Economic Community (1958 - see page 115). For post-war French economic policy had been rigorously protectionist while both the ECSC and the EEC were founded to encourage a free market in goods and services between their six member states. Here was a paradox, and one which worried French businessmen, many of whom advised the government not to enter the EEC because they feared that French industries would be undermined by competition from other EEC members like West Germany and Italy.

The case was finely balanced. Membership of the European organisations would provide access to a wider market of 180 millions, and sharpen the pressure for modernisation through foreign competition. But many businessmen and economists believed that France, with her growing balance of payments deficit and rising prices in the late 1950s, would not be able to meet the EEC demand that tariffs between member states should be eliminated within 12 to 15 years. There was a further stipulation that tariffs on imports from non-EEC states were to be reduced to the EEC average for 1958 which was below the normal French level. In 1958 the advantages of Western European integration seemed clear, but the disadvantages were equally obvious. Would traditionally protectionist France be able to adapt herself to the new free market Europe?

Agriculture seemed especially vulnerable. France had millions of small peasant farmers (although the percentage working on the land had been falling steadily since 1945) using outdated technology. It seemed likely that they would fall victim to the more efficient foreign farmers such as the Dutch. However, in this instance, tough French negotiating procured a Common Agricultural Policy for the EEC which provided farmers with guaranteed prices and income support. The CAP was increasingly advantageous to France, with her large farming sector, and became a bone of contention with fellow EEC states.

Other measures also helped the French economy to adapt to EEC membership. These were deflationary in emphasis involving such things as the end to indexation of prices and wages which had been an important component in French economic planning. Arguably, too, the emergence of a more decisive political leadership under General de Gaulle in 1958 prolonged the economic miracle into the 1960s, but it is important to recognise the economic achievement of the Fourth Republic. Political weakness does not inevitably lead to economic weakness.

12 The European Dimension

France's economic achievement also undoubtedly owed something to her involvement in the process of European integration after 1945. However in France, as elsewhere in Western Europe, there was a debate between those who favoured federalism - essentially a rapid movement towards European political union - and those who supported functionalism - a more cautious and pragmatic desire for an economic and customs union first.

In 1948 France joined the Council of Europe which was meant to prepare the way for a federal Europe, and in 1949 she integrated her forces with the rest of Western Europe, the USA and Canada in the North Atlantic Treaty Organisation. Before this, Jean Monnet, a pragmatist over Europe as over State planning, won a considerable victory for the functionalists with his conception of the scheme to unite or 'pool' the coal and steel resources of France and West Germany. This came to be known as the Schuman Plan, after Robert Schuman the then French Foreign Minister, but it was in every sense Monnet's brainchild. This led to the creation of the ECSC in 1951. The French declaration of May 1950 stated that:

1 Europe must be organised on a federal basis. A Franco-German union is an essential element in it ... The French government proposes to place the whole of Franco-German coal and steel production under an international Authority open to the 5 participation of Europe.

By the polling of basic production and the establishment of a new High Authority whose decisions will be binding on France, Germany and the countries that join them, this proposal will lay the first concrete foundations of the European Federation which is 10 indispensable to the maintenance of peace.

This declaration was not quite as altruistic as a superficial reading might suggest. The French were alarmed by the encouragement of West German rearmament by the USA (a response to an enhanced fear of communism when the Korean War started in 1950). This was not just a matter of fear of renewed German military power: this rearmament also threatened to consume the coking coal from the Ruhr on which French steel production relied. Anti-German sentiment began to rise in France again, and there were references to the *sales Boches* (dirty Germans) before the Schuman Plan defused the situation. It provided for a supranational authority to control both French and German coal and steel production, and ultimately that of Italy and the Benelux countries as well when the ECSC was formed. It was also true, of course, that the pooling of Franco-German resources made another war unlikely, and in this sense, the Schuman Plan was symptomatic of, in the words of the declaration, France and Germany's desire 'not to go to war with one another again'.

However, Franco-German suspicions did not entirely disappear with the foundation of the ECSC, for there was further controversy in 1954 over plans for a European Defence Community (EDC) and a European Political Community (EPC) which would include West Germany. The crucial struggle was over the EDC which would have involved giving authority over France's armed forces to a supranational authority. Worse, it would have meant being in a supranational European army with the Germans, when Britain had refused to join the EDC. Many French people regarded this as intolerable, although the EDC had its admirers, notably in the MRP.

Between 1952 and 1954 successive French governments were put under considerable pressure to ratify the EDC Treaty by the Americans who were keen (partly for financial reasons) that the Germans should play a part in the defence of Western Europe. However, until the advent of Mendés-France in 1954 French governments lacked the courage to put this divisive issue before Parliament. Mendés-France appears to have been lukewarm in his attitude to the EDC, preferring links with Britain to those with Germany, and being unenthusiastic about the sort of European union advocated by Monnet. Like many French nationals, he seems to have been concerned about the loss of sovereignty to a supra-national authority, which signing the EDC Treaty would mean. This might be acceptable in the economic sphere (as with the ECSC), but defence was a different matter, as joining the EDC would involve France giving up the control of her armed forces.

Did Mendés-France, as his political opponents suggested, set out deliberately to scupper the EDC Treaty from the outset? There is no conclusive evidence that he did, although a ministerial colleague suggested that he did so in exchange for Soviet approval of the Indo-China settlement at Geneva. The French Communists opposed the Treaty which they regarded as anti-Soviet, but there is no convincing evidence that Mendés-France was, as opponents said, trying to forge a new alliance with the USSR.

Indeed Mendés-France seems to have done his best to get the EDC Treaty through, although he was never confident that it would get the

Assembly's approval. He also went to Brussels in an attempt to modify the terms of the Treaty but the other potential members of EDC (Italy, the Benelux states, and West Germany) refused to meet Mendés' demands. Crucially for many members of the Assembly, Britain refused to join the EDC. Ultimately the Assembly decided by 319 votes to 264 to postpone discussion of the EDC indefinitely. This decision in August 1954 effectively killed off the EDC. The plan for a European Political Union went down with it, despite the known US support for both the EPC and the EDC.

What was the significance for France of the failure of the EDC proposal? In the short term, it did Mendés-France little good, because the strongly pro-European MRP never forgave him for, in their eyes, not pushing the Treaty hard enough. But more importantly, it committed France to the more pragmatic, slower route to European unity enshrined in the Treaty of Rome in 1957.

13 De Gaulle and Algeria

The last years of the Fourth Republic were overshadowed by the colonial war in Algeria which started in 1954 and which caused bitter division within France. Although Mendés-France had conceded independence to neighbouring Tunisia, Algeria was a different matter. Not only was it the oldest of France's colonies in North Africa but it was also the only colony to have a large French settler population - the one million *pieds noirs* (literally 'black feet', the nickname given to the settlers by the Arabs).

Apart from the native Algerian revolt led by the Front de Libération Nationale (National Liberation Front), the French situation was made infinitely more difficult by the vehemence of the *pieds noirs* opposition to any suggestion of independence for Algeria. Successive governments were, in fact, intimidated by the *colons* (colonists) who showed their strength of feeling by throwing missiles at the Socialist Prime Minister, Guy Mollet, when he visited Algeria in 1956. It was Mollet who, in a mistaken belief that the Egyptian leader Nasser was supplying the Algerian rebels, got France involved in the ill-fated Suez adventure in the same year which failed to bring Nasser down.

By 1958 the situation had reached crisis point when the *pieds noirs* and a rebel element in the French army suspected that the then government was going to negotiate with the FLN. Paratroopers in Algiers were in a state of revolt against the government and threatened invasion of mainland France. The government in Paris was in a state of panic, while the rebel army generals appealed to de Gaulle to save 'French Algeria'. As the republican government had no idea how to solve the crisis, it was by no means unhappy to turn matters over to the General once more. So it was that on 28 May 1958 de Gaulle got 'the call' which he had waited 12 years to receive. As Prime Minister his first move was to demand a restoration of military discipline in Algeria, and this he was able to accomplish because of the authority he possessed both as a military man and as the former Head of the Free French.

The evidence concerning de Gaulle's long-term intentions about Algeria is contradictory. He visited Algeria in June 1958 and received a tumultuous welcome from the *pieds noirs*. In his memoirs de Gaulle wrote: 'In Constantine, where the audience was principally Moslem, in Oran, where the French were largely predominant, in Mostagnem, where the two communities were evenly balanced, my message was the same.' This account is contradicted in Lacouture's definitive biography which notes that at Mostagnem, unlike in the other cities, de Gaulle cried *'Vive l'Algerie Française'* (Long live French Algeria). The ambiguity is increased by de Gaulle's own comment to an aide shortly afterwards that the *pieds noirs* were 'dreaming. They're forgetting that there are nine million Muslims to one million Europeans', a comment which suggested that Algerian independence was inevitable. Did the General, therefore, create the illusion that he would stand by the French Algerians for tactical reasons until his power base was secure enough in France for him to move towards an accommodation with the FLN rebels?

It was a profound historical irony that General de Gaulle, who was the most trenchant critic of the Fourth Republic was now to preside over its death throes. First, he served as Prime Minister over a government of all the parties (except the Communists) and some technical specialists, and then set about establishing the new constitution which he had always wanted. This was approved by the French people on 18

De Gaulle and reconstruction	The Economy The plan EEC membership
The emergence of the Fourth Republic Party politics	Colonial problems Indo-China Algeria
Challenges to the Republic Communism Gaullism Poujadism	Foreign policy The Schuman Plan ECSC, EPC, EDC, EEC

Summary - The Fourth Republic, 1946-58

September 1958 with a massive 75 per cent 'yes' vote, and provided for just the powerful executive presidency that de Gaulle had wanted and failed to get in 1946. Meantime, until his new constitution became operative in January 1959, de Gaulle ruled France by emergency decree without reference to parliament. It said much about his stormy relationship with the dying Fourth Republic that at the transfer of power ceremony the General snubbed the outgoing President whose toothless office he had so despised.

Making notes on *'The Fourth Republic, 1946-58'*

In making your notes on this period, concentrate on the six major aspects, as identified in the summary diagram on page 118, and how they interlink. This period is unique in modern French history because of the high profile of colonial problems and their influence on the politics of the time. The following headings should give you a framework for your notes.

1   Reconstruction
1.1 The evolution of the constitution.
1.2 Economic recovery.
1.3 De Gaulle's retirement.
2   Party politics
2.1 The Search for stability.
2.2 The PCF and the RPF.
2.3 The Third Force.
2.4 Mendésisme.
2.5 Poujadism.
3   The Fall of the Republic
3.1 The economic miracle.
3.2 Foreign policy.
3.3 Algeria.
3.4 The return of de Gaulle.

Answering essay questions on *'The Fourth Republic, 1946-58'*

This chapter has covered some very big themes: post-war recovery, decolonisation and France's involvement in the European movement. They are often closely interlinked and are very complex. It can be difficult to 'see the wood for the trees' but again it may help to put essay titles under separate headings. Study these questions:

Constitutional Reform and Economic Recovery
1   Why did Charles de Gaulle succeed in giving France an executive presidency in 1958 when he had failed to do so in 1946?

2   Outline the characteristics of post-war French economic policy and account for France's economic miracle in the 1950s.
3   Why was the PCF excluded from government after 1947?

Decolonisation
4   Why did a colonial revolt begin in Indo-China in 1946 and why did France fail to suppress it?
5   Explain the origins and internal consequences of the Algerian War

Foreign Affairs
6   Why did the relationship with West Germany dominate France's external relations between 1949 and 1955?

The unique feature of this period, and the start of the Gaullist period which followed it is the dominant role played by long and bloody colonial wars, but both had considerable internal ramifications. Both Question 3 and especially Question 5, demand awareness of the linkage between domestic and colonial policy.

Source-based questions on 'The Fourth Republic, 1946-58'

1 General de Gaulle's Resignation, 1946
Study the extract from de Gaulle's memoirs on page 100 and his remarks on page 103. Then answer the following questions.
a) In what way does de Gaulle suggest that he had already thought about retiring from politics before 1946? (3 marks)
b) In both extracts, what reasons does de Gaulle give for disapproving of the state of French politics? (5 marks)
c) What evidence does the first source contain to explain de Gaulle's statement that 'my mission is ended'? (5 marks)
d) In what ways do the two extracts differ in their explanation for de Gaulle's behaviour in 1946? (7 marks)

2 The Franco-German Declaration, 1950
Study the extract on page 115 and answer the following questions.
a) What do you understand by the phrase 'on a federal basis'? (2 marks)
b) What, according to the source, was the purpose of the Franco-German declaration? (6 marks)
c) Use the material in the extract and your own knowledge to show how the Schuman Plan contributed to the integration of Western Europe. (7 marks)

CHAPTER 7

The Fifth Republic, 1958-69

In a manner unparalleled in twentieth-century French history, the story of the Fifth Republic between 1958 and 1969 is dominated by one man - Charles de Gaulle - and his philosophy of government.

1 De Gaulle's Background

Charles de Gaulle was born in 1890 to a strongly Catholic, royalist family. His father was a history teacher and it was from him that the young de Gaulle got his strong sense of the past, as well as an individualistic streak. He went into the army, graduated from the celebrated military academy of Saint Cyr, and served with some distinction in the First World War. De Gaulle was, therefore, preeminently a soldier, but he was also an intellectual who made a reputation for himself as a lecturer at the *École de Guerre* (War School) in the inter-war period, and was familiar with all the great works of French literature. But, above all, he was a patriot with an unwavering belief in French greatness and a 'certain idea of France', and this tendency came to the fore when he rallied the Free French forces around him after France's traumatic defeat by Germany in 1940. At this time he was a little known general who had fled to England and had been condemned to death in his absence by the collaborationist Vichy regime.

Throughout the war years, when his country was occupied by the Germans and the Vichyites, de Gaulle fought hard to establish a role for the Free French among far stronger allies (Britain and the USA) who did not always appreciate his independence of mind or his prickly French nationalism. Not for nothing did Churchill describe the General as 'my cross of Lorraine' (the cross of Lorraine was the emblem of the Free French movement).

De Gaulle never forgot those wartime experiences and they are central to any understanding of his policies, for he refused to let France be dominated by other powers after his return to office in 1958. In the same way his experience as leader of the post-war Provisional Government between 1944 and 1946 was crucial too (see page 99). It both heightened his suspicion of party politicians, and strengthened his belief in the need for a strong executive presidency. This was the price he extracted for his return to French politics in May 1958.

2 Gaullism

Charles de Gaulle was associated with a body of ideas which became known as 'Gaullism', although he always denied that Gaullism was in any sense a doctrine or an ideology. He wrote in his war memoirs:

1 All my life I have had a certain idea of France. It has been inspired
as much by sentiment as by reason. The emotional side of me
imagines France, like the princess in the fairy stories or the
madonna in the frescoes, as dedicated to an exalted and
5 exceptional destiny. Instinctively I have the feeling that Providence
has created her for complete success or exemplary misfortunes. If,
in spite of this, mediocrity shows in her acts and deeds, it strikes me
as an absurd anomaly imputable to the faults of the French not the
genius of the country. But the positive side of my mind also
10 convinces me that France is not really herself except in the front
rank; that only vast enterprises are capable of counterbalancing the
ferment of dispersion that our people carries in itself; that our
country, such as it is, among others, such as they are, must aim
high and hold itself straight, on pain of mortal danger. In short, to
15 my mind, France cannot be France without greatness.

What does this passage tell us about de Gaulle's philosophy? Most
notably, that for him foreign affairs must dominate because France must
be in 'the first rank'. If Gaullism was to be about anything it was, as one
historian has said, about the politics of grandeur. This is not to say that
there was not to be a strong link between foreign and domestic policy in
the early years of the Fifth Republic, for de Gaulle tried to secure his
position at home by giving France a distinctive voice in world affairs,
which would make French men and women proud and incline them to
support his regime. There is a French saying that *un régime c'est d'abord
un style'* (a regime is above everything a style), and under de Gaulle the
Fifth Republic had a very distinctive style. It was authoritarian and
remote at home, and proud and independent in its dealings with foreign
countries. Critics of de Gaulle argued that there was more style than
substance in his regime, and that it was very much a one-man band with
the General's influence to be seen everywhere. Central to de Gaulle's
beliefs was a distaste, referred to in the last chapter, for institutions and
groups which got in the way of his relationship with the nation. He was
fond of using the phrase 'the depths of the nation' (*'la nation profonde'*)
with which he believed he had a unique relationship. Anything, be it
politicians or Parliament, which got in the way of this relationship with
the people, was regarded with a degree of contempt. Hence de Gaulle's
preference after 1958 for referenda, votes of the mass of the French
people which missed out the tiresome parliamentary process of general
elections.

It could be argued, therefore, that de Gaulle's beliefs were
characteristic of a man with a Catholic, royalist background and a
military training. Yet de Gaulle, during his two spells in political office
(1944-6 and 1958-69), never sought to make himself a dictator, which
he certainly could have done during the second period. Nothing about
de Gaulle was ever simple.

After 1958 de Gaulle was to lobby at home for 'participation' of French workers in the management of industry, although he was singularly vague about how this was to be done. He disliked the idea of the Left-Right split in French politics, yet he clearly relied on the newly established right-wing Gaullist party to keep him in power. At times he could appear almost childishly naive while retaining a capacity to be both ruthless and cunning. In the last analysis it may be true that Gaullism was little more than de Gaulle 'writ large', strongly nationalistic but offering no coherent political doctrine to help in solving France's problems in the 1950s and 1960s. Instead, de Gaulle offered his almost mystical belief that he could hold French society together.

3 The Constitutional Reforms

The constitutional reforms (see also page 118) which de Gaulle introduced in 1958-9 expressed to a degree the ambivalence present at the heart of Gaullism and the newly-founded Fifth Republic. De Gaulle had always wanted a strong executive presidency, which would avoid the unseemly party bickering which had been characteristic of the Fourth Republic. Superficially the constitution of the Fifth Republic seemed to do this by making Cabinet ministers no longer responsible to Parliament. Indeed it removed the need for ministers even to be elected as parliamentary Deputies, for as soon as a Deputy was made a member of the government he had to resign his seat and be replaced by a substitute. In addition, the constitution removed the need constantly to obtain parliamentary approval for government actions by assuming that such approval existed unless a vote of censure was passed in Parliament against the government of the day. But in the last analysis, governments in the Fifth Republic do need ultimate parliamentary approval for their actions. If this is not obtained, the government could be overturned by a majority vote of censure in the Chamber of Deputies, and the drafters of the constitution made it clear that in their minds Parliament should be paramount. It included a phrase describing Parliament as 'determining and conducting policy'.

From the start there was ambivalence about who really runs France under the Fifth Republic. This was partly to do with the personality of de Gaulle himself who wrote haughtily: 'Whoever believed that General de Gaulle ought to content himself with opening chrysanthemum shows?' It was also to do with the undoubted strengthening of presidential powers under the new constitution, for now the President could dissolve the Chamber of Deputies, appeal directly to the French people over Parliament's head by means of referenda, and use Article 16 to declare a national emergency and rule without Parliament.

A further adjustment took place in 1962 when de Gaulle secured a constitutional amendment, after a referendum, which made the President electable by the French people. Previously this had been the responsibility of 80,000 notable citizens of the Republic. This move certainly seemed insulting to Parliament, for never before in the twentieth century had a constitutional change been made without parliamentary approval, and on this occasion, de Gaulle's supporters in the Assembly lost a vote of censure. But de Gaulle ignored this and blackmailed the electorate into approving the amendment by saying that if the referendum on it was lost, he would resign. Yet again de Gaulle seemed to be trying to ignore the parliamentary process and reaching out to 'the depths of the nation', although direct election of the President was obviously more democratic.

There was nevertheless still confusion about exactly what the constitutional reforms were supposed to achieve, for it is clear that on one level de Gaulle was well aware that Parliament should be the final arbiter. Otherwise it is hard to explain his invention of the so-called 'reserved domain', that is those areas of government policy such as foreign policy and defence which were to be left to presidential control (in practice, de Gaulle managed at times to interfere in all areas of government policy). It would not have been necessary to invent such a doctrine if de Gaulle was not afraid that Parliament could impinge on the running of foreign affairs and defence policy. He further muddied the constitutional waters by saying in 1964 that the President had the 'indivisible authority of the state' while the Prime Minister dealt with the day-to-day running of the government.

What did this mean? In practice little, because de Gaulle continued to meddle on a day-to-day basis with the running of the country. Worse, he felt able to sack Debré as Prime Minister in 1962, when the latter had merely indicated that in his view parliamentary elections should follow the important Algerian settlement, and in 1968 he removed Georges Pompidou who had (in the General's view) become too popular and independent minded. The constitutional changes of 1958, therefore, may not have been designed to create an over-mighty President, but as operated by de Gaulle, they seemed to do just that. Too often the line between electoral dictatorship (through referenda) and real democracy became blurred.

However, a central paradox remains about the period 1958 to 1969. Ostensibly, France remained a highly authoritarian state in which ministers could read about government decisions in the newspapers, and the government-controlled TV could announce when de Gaulle was abroad 'in the absence of General de Gaulle there is no political news today'. But the government still needed a majority in Parliament and de Gaulle, despite his longstanding dislike of political parties, found himself the leader of one. In reality de Gaulle was forced to play coalition politics because only once, in 1968, did the Gaullists have an absolute majority in the Chamber of Deputies. Otherwise they had to rely on the support in Parliament of the small right-wing Independent Republicans or the centre-right MRP.

Throughout the de Gaulle period, therefore, and despite the constitutional reforms, French politics was riddled with paradoxes. Its head of state had no ambition to be a dictator, and ultimately resigned from office in 1969, yet frequently behaved in a highly authoritarian manner. This authoritarianism then pervaded the rest of French society.

France was a parliamentary democracy but de Gaulle ignored a vote of censure in Parliament (albeit there was only one between 1958 and 1969), and sacked prime ministers on little more than a personal whim. The device of the referendum was also abused in France to a degree unknown since the days of Napoleon III in the nineteenth century. Every time major issues arose, de Gaulle appealed to the French people over the head of Parliament. This made the alterations to the constitution of the Republic in 1958 almost irrelevant. The exact balance between Parliament and the presidency did not matter when de Gaulle was constantly using referenda.

Yet ultimately, de Gaulle built better than he knew, for the politics of the Fifth Republic have been more stable than that of its predecessor, and its institutions survived that ultimate horror (in the eyes of Gaullists), the victory of the Left in 1981. The question remains, however, of whether once the Algerian emergency was over, de Gaulle's authoritarian regime could be justified in a country which claimed, after all, to be a democracy.

4 The Algerian Question

French politics was dominated between 1958 and 1962 by one issue - Algeria. It was the issue which had brought de Gaulle to power, and it was the only one which could have brought him down before his voluntary retirement from politics in 1969. Algeria also had the potential to bring about civil war in France, and the effects of the emergency did make her the victim of urban terrorism in the early 1960s.

Chapter 6 referred to both General de Gaulle's caution and his ambivalence over the Algerian Question. Four days after he came to power in May 1958, de Gaulle visited Algiers (one of five visits that year) and told the *pieds noirs,* 'I have understood you'. This ambivalent utterance was received with frantic enthusiasm by the *colons* (colonists) but no-one noticed that the only positive element in the speech was the reference to electoral equality for the Muslim majority in Algeria. In June 1958 de Gaulle made his one and only reference to 'French Algeria' (see page 118), but in October he reverted to masterful double-meaning by crying 'long live Algeria with France, long live France with Algeria'. As one historian has pointed out, this was not the same thing at all.

Can we find a key to de Gaulle's intentions in his memoirs (admittedly written long after the event)? There de Gaulle wrote that he had no 'predetermined plan' although he claimed that he was already, in

1958, convinced of Algeria's right to self-determination. De Gaulle also wrote, 'I had to manoeuvre without ever changing course using each crisis as an opportunity to go further'. This has to be taken with a large pinch of salt because, as the historian Julian Jackson remarked in his study of de Gaulle, the French leader 'manoeuvred so successfully that it is impossible to know what exactly he originally intended'. Historians have detected different nuances in de Gaulle's policy, whereby for Jackson it was 'a learning process' with de Gaulle reacting to various setbacks, while for James MacMillan the Algerian policy was one of 'wait and see'. By contrast, Williams and Harrison have seen the attitude of the army as crucial, with de Gaulle's ambivalent statements to be explained by his need to mollify the military. The army had, after all, suffered a humiliating defeat in Indo-China in 1954, and did not wish to repeat the experience.

Whatever the explanation for de Gaulle's policy may be, there were distinctive stages in its evolution. De Gaulle came to power on a wave of popular approval in Algeria from the *pieds noirs,* and it took him some time (despite what he said in his memoirs) to come out fully in favour of Algerian independence. For about two years he tried to find a middle way between the extreme *pieds noirs* on one side, and the FLN on the other. Thus, in October 1958, he made a proposal for a five-year investment plan to provide educational and economic opportunities for Muslims, and the famous 'peace of the brave' offer to the FLN. This was denounced by the FLN as tantamount to surrender, and the Muslims also boycotted the local elections in Algeria.

This setback was followed by nine months of deadlock until October 1959 when de Gaulle announced that in his view Algeria's long-term future lay in 'self-determination', but the French President's offer to the Algerians was circumscribed by what he thought most appropriate for them. There were, in de Gaulle's view, three choices: 1) so-called 'francisation' whereby Algeria would be integrated with France, 2) secession from France, 3) self-government in association with France. It was clear that de Gaulle was extremely hostile to the second option, and the long-term nature of this Algerian proposal was made evident by the rider that a referendum on the future in both Algeria and metropolitan France would only be held five years after the return of peace. Faced with these terms it was not surprising that the FLN rejected de Gaulle's appeal for a ceasefire. However, despite this setback, some historians have still seen the offer of October 1959 as a key moment in the evolution of de Gaulle's Algerian policy. He made clear his preference for the third option of Algerian self-government in association with France, but did at least envisage the possibility of independence at some stage in the future.

Certainly in doing so de Gaulle lost any support he may have had among the European settlers in Algeria. In January 1960 the *pieds noirs* revolted and occupied key buildings in Algiers in what was known as the 'week of the barricades'. As they were helped by some army units there seemed to be a real danger that de Gaulle might be overthrown. In the event, he defused the crisis with a memorable TV appeal for army loyalty. But he was sufficiently worried by the situation to go on a 'tour of the messes' (that is the army units) in March 1960. De Gaulle reassured the soldiers that they would not suffer defeat as they had done in Indo-China, a hard-line position which did not really equate with his conversion to the principle of an independent Algeria. Clearly the loyalty of the army was a priority at the time.

De Gaulle's subsequent behaviour after the abortive revolt in 1960 has caused him to be criticised for deviousness because he seemed at one point to be seriously negotiating with a dissident faction of the FLN. These overtures failed, but they may have been part of an attempt to force the FLN into peace talks by encouraging divisions in its ranks. As it was, French insistence on a ceasefire before substantive talks with the FLN were unacceptable to that organisation.

Slowly but surely thereafter, de Gaulle's position developed. By November 1960 he was talking about 'the Algerian republic which will

General de Gaulle speaks to the nation on television, 26 April 1961

exist one day', and in January 1961 he announced that a referendum would take place to approve the principle of self-determination before a ceasefire. A month earlier he had endured a hostile reception in Algiers but with characteristic bravery had insisted on shaking hands with supporters in the crowds. A further consequence of that visit had been that he had finally convinced himself of the inevitability of independence because of the level of mass support for the FLN.

When the referendum was held in 1961 it gave de Gaulle a massive endorsement (75.26 per cent voted 'yes') although in Algiers the *pieds noirs* registered a 72 per cent vote against him. This result gave him the popular mandate he needed to open talks with the FLN.

It was also the last straw for those elements in the French military who could not tolerate the idea of an end to 'French Algeria', and in April 1961 the same group of generals who had brought de Gaulle back to power in May 1958 staged a military uprising in Algiers. Once again de Gaulle remained calm and made a crucial TV broadcast which was scornful of the rebels and won over army support in Algeria (unlike his Prime Minister Debré who panicked and made a hysterical broadcast asking citizens to block runways with their cars lest France be invaded by paratroopers from Algeria). This was the last time elements in the Army challenged de Gaulle's authority and the ringleaders were arrested. Crucially, public opinion in France itself, excepting only the far Right, gave its President overwhelming support at this moment of crisis.

Formal talks with the FLN then began at Evian in May with de Gaulle showing a desire to get out of Algeria as soon as possible. Nevertheless, the negotiation process did take a further ten months before a settlement was reached. This was for two reasons: first, the issue of what was to happen to the *pieds noirs* remained; second, the French wished to retain the Algerian Sahara with its extensive oil deposits. Ultimately de Gaulle was forced to accept that there could be no special deal for the *pieds noirs,* and that the oil deposits would be under Algerian control.

It was during this period of negotiation that the extremist *pieds noirs* made their last strike at de Gaulle through the terrorist organisation, the OAS (Secret Army Organisation). It carried out bombings in both France and Algeria and made several attempts on de Gaulle's life (during one in August 1962 de Gaulle miraculously survived his car being riddled with 14 bullets), but it had minimal support outside Algeria. Peace ultimately came for Algeria in the Evian Accords of March 1962, and with it the end of the most severe emergency faced by the Fifth Republic.

Historians have generally recognised the nature of de Gaulle's achievement in making the Algerian settlement. Indeed his contemporary, the Chinese leader Mao Zedong, stated that no other world leader could have brought off such a deal. But one of his biographers (Jean Lacouture) has accused him of being in too much of a hurry in trying to end the Algerian emergency. By contrast, Jackson believes that a more realistic approach over the issues of the *pieds noirs* and the Saharan deposits would have ended the Algerian war even sooner. As outlined above, de Gaulle has been accused of deviousness because of his various shifts of policy between 1958 and 1962.

Are these criticisms valid? It is certainly true that de Gaulle took two years to reach a position where he accepted the inevitability of Algerian independence, but the pressures on him were enormous. In particular, the attitude of the army, until the failure of the April 1961 coup, was uncertain, and de Gaulle had to manoeuvre between *pieds noirs* hostility and a growing anti-war movement in France.

De Gaulle himself was aggravated by the knowledge that the Algerian issue was distracting him from others equally important for France's future (as he himself said 'Algeria blocks everything'). So he was in a hurry to achieve a settlement, and it can be argued that knowledge of this fact put the FLN enemy at an advantage in the negotiating process. But who else had the stature and the prestige to win over the army, the Muslims in Algeria, and the vast mass of the French population? This achievement, too, as historians have pointed out, was the work of a man who by upbringing was very much an admirer of France's imperial tradition, and confessed himself saddened by the loss of Algeria. Thus, although it is possible to argue that de Gaulle was variously too slow and too quick in his efforts to resolve the Algerian problem, it is hard to deny the importance of the achievement itself. In the end, too, a streak of ruthlessness showed itself in his apparent unconcern for the fate of the *pieds noirs* (most of whom fled to France) or the harkis, those Muslims who had fought on the French side in the eight-year war (many of whom were massacred by the FLN). But then the General always argued that, while an individual could have friends, a nation could not.

5 The Domestic Front

De Gaulle never disguised the fact that foreign affairs were his main interest. Foreign policy after all was the sphere where the 'politics of grandeur' could be displayed to best effect. However, he could make decisive interventions from time to time in domestic affairs.

a) The Economy

De Gaulle never professed to be an economist, but he did have a decisive say on economic matters on two occasions. Soon after coming to power in December 1958 he insisted on the imposition of the Rueff-Pinay plan (named after a conservative economist and the then Finance Minister, who was far from enthusiastic about it). This was designed to halve the inflationary spiral which had so weakened the Fourth Republic, and involved cuts in public expenditure, devaluation of the franc, and an end to restrictions on foreign trade. In fact the policy proved to be very successful, until a build-up of inflation reoccurred in 1963. In order to counteract this de Gaulle persuaded another reluctant finance minister, Giscard d'Estaing, to introduce credit restrictions, but France did go through a minor slump between 1964 and 1966. Nevertheless, economic growth in France during the de Gaulle years was impressive.

It was a paradox, therefore, that it was in the economic sphere that de Gaulle's government was most vulnerable. This was because some sectors of French society did not share in the overall prosperity, notably the peasantry who demonstrated against the government in 1960-1. There was also a damaging miners' strike in 1963 which was badly handled by a government which attempted to force the miners back to work, and then had to back down. It was significant that opinion polls showed that de Gaulle's popularity reached its lowest point in 1963 (with 42 per cent dissatisfied and only 40 per cent satisfied).

This dissatisfaction was reflected in the presidential election of 1965 when de Gaulle achieved only a narrow victory over François Mitterrand, the candidate of the Left (presidential elections had to be held every seven years). In general the President paid little attention to this evidence of economic discontent, although he preached a doctrine of modernisation. Some small concessions were made to popular discontent over the economy, but by and large the General was too absorbed with foreign policy imperatives to pay very much attention to it. Yet polls showed consistent discontent with the economy between 1964 and 1969, even though there was clear evidence that the average French person became better off during the period. De Gaulle seemed to be better at restoring people's national pride (a vague emotion at the best of times) than at convincing them of their economic well-being.

How do we account for this economic discontent? Answers can really only be speculative. The end of the Algerian war (which had been very costly) and France's entry into the EEC (see page 115) may have raised expectations, but it is hard to explain why dissatisfaction with the regime was reflected in the economic sphere rather than in the political one where de Gaulle had achieved an unhealthy domination.

b) The 'Events' of May 1968

Other than the various crises over Algeria the major challenge to de Gaulle took place in May 1968 when, for a few heady days, students and workers united in massive demonstrations against the regime. Historians have debated the issues behind the 'events' *(les evénéments)* of 1968 ever since.

The events of 1968 took place in a context of growing disillusionment with both de Gaulle and his regime. Even the General himself seemed to sense this when he bemoaned the fact that there was nothing 'heroic' left to do. The elections of 1967 underlined this mood when the Gaullist party (UNR) lost seats in the parliamentary elections (this followed de Gaulle's poor showing in the presidential election of 1965).

There were two distinct strands to the 1968 uprising. The motor for disturbance was provided by the students who were embittered by high failure rates and overcrowded accommodation (in 1938-9 France had only 60,000 in higher education, but by 1967-8 this figure had risen to 605,000). This was combined with a degree of far-Left Trotskyite influence on a hard core of student activists, led by a German national Daniel Cohn-Bendit (popularly known as 'Danny the Red'). But the physical environment in which students had to live played a crucial role in precipitating the 'events' of 1968. It was no accident that the student revolt started in the soulless concrete campus at Nanterre (a Paris suburb) which did not even have a proper library. Right-wing commentators also thought it significant that Nanterre had a large sociology department.

Basic student grievances were combined with the universal cause of Vietnam, where the presence of American troops sparked off student disturbances throughout Europe. In France there was a bombing campaign against American property in Paris. When a Nanterre student was implicated in the bombings and arrested, it provided the touch paper for the violence that followed. In March the administration closed the Nanterre campus, and in May all teaching was suspended there after violent incidents.

The action then moved to the Sorbonne campus in the middle of Paris where support for the Nanterre students had begun to grow. At this point the Rector of the Sorbonne, probably fearing Left-Right violence on the campus, called in the police to prevent it. This was a fatal error. The CRS riot police in France have never been noted for finesse, and they used batons and tear gas to brutal effect on student demonstrators. The whole situation escalated out of control and more than 500 people were injured in the fighting. For ten days in May 1968 France was traumatised by the sight of student rioters and riot police doing battle.

The government announced that teaching at the Sorbonne was suspended, but this only provoked worse violence on 10-11 May in which cars were burnt, Molotov cocktails (petrol bombs) were thrown at the police, and some 400 students were arrested. The outside world which watched these battles on TV was horrified by the readiness with which the CRS battered rioting students and innocent bystanders (including Red Cross workers) alike. In France itself police brutality became an issue and did much to arouse working-class support for the students. It was this workers' involvement that made the events in France distinct from similar student agitation in the USA, West Germany and Britain.

The large-scale, working-class involvement was the second strand in the 'events' of 1968, but from the outset the workers had their own agenda which involved getting better pay and conditions. Neither was Paris itself the centre of working-class agitation, a fact all too easily forgotten afterwards when the events of 1968 were often presented as having been Paris-centred. In fact the agitation began first of all in the aircraft factory at Nantes, and then at the Renault car plant near Rouen (both places in Normandy).

Working-class grievances in 1968 were essentially economic. Low wages were combined with oppressive industrial discipline, so that workers had virtually no say in the management of their factories. Unemployment was high amongst the young and unskilled and there was growing disillusionment with traditional trade union structures like the CGT which failed to improve conditions, or wages. The workers' slogan in 1968 was 'participation'. This was a demand not just for more money but to be heard and valued by both the state and the employers. Even professional groups such as doctors took up the demand for 'participation'.

To begin with, an illusion of student-worker unity was created (best shown in a massive 750,000 strong demonstration on 13 May), but it did not last. Student militants like Cohn-Bendit wanted revolution and a Trotskyite paradise, while the workers' demands were essentially practical. Once elements in the government recognised this the illusion of unity was easily punctured by making concessions to the workers.

However, de Gaulle himself did not recognise this. Indeed he seemed paralysed by the sight of the agitation, made an ineffective TV broadcast, and on 29 May 'disappeared'. In fact, he went to Germany to the headquarters of the parachute general Massu, a veteran of Indo-China and Algeria who commanded part of France's contribution to West Germany's defence. Myths have grown up about exactly what did happen on that day. According to one version, de Gaulle greeted Massu with the phrase *'C'est foutu'* (It's finished) and had to be persuaded to return to France, after apparently losing his nerve. Another has it that de Gaulle's disappearance was a brilliant tactical diversion, designed to show the French people how indispensable he was. The evidence is inconclusive, but it is known that de Gaulle originally wanted to meet Massu in eastern France but could not communicate this wish to his headquarters. Conversely, de Gaulle is alleged to have said to Madame Massu, 'It was providence that placed your husband in my path on May 29' (the inference being that Massu had indeed persuaded the shaken President to return to France).

Whatever the truth of the matter, de Gaulle returned to France and on 30 May made a robust speech on TV in which he cleverly played on right-wingers' fear of communism (it did not matter that the French Communist Party had denounced the student radicals). But the man who really defeated the student radicals was the Prime Minister Georges Pompidou who detached them from their working-class allies by means of the Grenelles Agreements. These gave the workers wage increases of 10 per cent or more, together with family and old-age benefits and a reduction in the working week. His reward for steering the government towards salvation was to be sacked as Prime Minister (he held the post from 1962 to 1968) and to be replaced by the Gaullist stooge, Maurice Couve de Murville. But when in June 1968 the Gaullists for the first time won an outright majority in Parliament, there was little doubt that it was Pompidou's victory more than his master's. De Gaulle's prestige had been fatally shaken by the May events, which he did not foresee, because for French youth he was a remote, paternalist figure. Even the comparatively conservative young people of France (who, it has been pointed out, mostly lived at home with their parents and preferred Françoise Hardy and Johnny Hallyday to the more non- conformist Rolling Stones and Beatles!), had tired of de Gaulle's pretensions. However, their parents showed even more forcibly in the June elections that they would not surrender the economic gains of the 1960s for some left-wing utopia.

What essentially were the events of 1968 all about? One view put forward by historians such as Robert Aron and Richard Cobb was that May 1968 was in no sense a serious revolutionary event but a 'psychodrama', the work of indulgent exhibitionist students who flirted with far-Left ideas, but had no radical vision of French society. The French historian Goubert supports this view and refers to Cohn-Bendit's followers as 'hoodlums' who burnt cars, while a British counterpart, Bernard Ledwidge, has seen les evénéments as part of the social movement of the 1960s towards sexual rather than political radicalism. An alternative view is that the discontent of May 1968 was real enough, and that a revolutionary situation was created by de Gaulle's dramatic disappearance on 19 May when the regime could have been toppled. The workers had shown, according to this line of argument, that they were thoroughly discontented with a regime which sponsored soulless automatism in the factories. But, if a revolutionary situation was created in May 1968, why was there no revolution? Primarily it seems, if we accept the argument that a revolutionary situation existed, because the working-class organisations, the PCF and the unions were so hostile to the student radicals. The communists bitterly denounced the students as 'fascist provocateurs' with no real interest in the workers, and in the end, the workers themselves were more concerned about economic concessions than with revolutionary change.

A middle position is taken by James MacMillan who argues that the crisis of May 1968 'undeniably was a real one, but it was neither as great as the student revolutionaries made out nor yet as slight as the Communists claimed'. MacMillan further argues that the opposition provided no real alternative to Gaullism, and that even had de Gaulle remained in Germany in a state of nervous breakdown, Pompidou who was the real saviour of the government would have preserved law and order. For Julian Jackson, the disturbances of 1968 were a revolt against the 'Republic of Silence' which he describes as 'a stultifyingly centralized and authoritarian system'. De Gaulle, who had tried to make a theatre out of politics, found himself the victim of political theatre as practised by the student protest movement. His histrionic offer to resign in the TV speech fiasco of 24 May was an example of this political theatricality, and it was the sober and practical Georges Pompidou who was left to sort out the mess.

The truth may lie between the two extremes. 'The events' had a greater significance than the French establishment, which included the Communist Party, was prepared to concede. But there is a difference between riots and revolution.

6 Foreign Policy

The point has been made earlier in this chapter that de Gaulle was pre-eminently concerned with foreign policy and that he had a special vision of French 'greatness'. As far as international affairs were concerned this meant finding France a new global role, even if de Gaulle's critics sometimes felt that this role involved making a great deal of noise about nothing.

Apart from his presumption of French greatness - indeed possibly even because of it - de Gaulle rejected the so-called bi-polar system which dominated international affairs after 1945. This system revolved around the domination of the world by the two superpowers, the USA and the USSR. De Gaulle flatly rejected superpower pretensions. He did not accept American leadership of the Western European alliance through the North Atlantic Treaty (founded in 1949). Neither did he accept the domination of Eastern Europe by the USSR. These were essentials in de Gaulle's European policy. But he also expected France to play a distinctive role in the extra-European world, a role to which he believed she was well suited because of her imperial past.

a) Defence Policy

De Gaulle's nationalistic policy was made evident by his decision to remove France from the NATO command structure in 1966, although she continued to co-operate with NATO states in defence planning. He also insisted that France should develop her own nuclear deterrent, and rejoiced when France exploded her first atomic bomb in 1960. This led to the setting up of the independent French nuclear bomber force known as the *force de frappe* (strike-force) in the 1960s. In nuclear terms, the French deterrent was puny, and arguably far too costly as well. But de Gaulle justified it by saying that because the USA had lost its nuclear monopoly in 1949 (when the USSR had exploded its first nuclear device), it would not risk nuclear annihilation by intervening in a war between the West and the USSR in Europe. In effect de Gaulle was saying that he did not trust the Americans to defend Western Europe, because they would always put their own interests first. 'It is intolerable,' said de Gaulle, 'that a great state should confide its destiny to the decision and action of another state, however friendly it may be.'

Therefore France must have her own independent deterrent which, he argued, however small it was, would deter the USSR because any nuclear attack on its territory by France would cause unacceptable damage. Similarly France had to put her own national interest first, and de Gaulle refused to sign the 1963 Test Ban Treaty (which banned nuclear testing in the atmosphere) because it would prevent the French advancing their technology and confirm the nuclear domination of the USA, USSR and Britain. It has to be conceded that de Gaulle's defence had widespread support across the political spectrum in France.

b) European Policy

De Gaulle's defence policy linked up with his European policy. He talked of a 'European Europe' which, as one historian points out, was confusing because it contained two apparently opposing strands. On the one hand, de Gaulle wished to strengthen France's links with Western Europe as he made clear in his memoirs:

1 My policy therefore aimed at the setting of a concert of European States which in developing all sorts of ties between them would increase their interdependence and solidarity. From this starting point, there was every reason to believe that the process of
5 evolution might lead to their confederation, especially if they were one day to be threatened from the same source. In practice this led us to put the European Economic Community into effect; to encourage the Six to concert together regularly in political matters.

On the other hand, he spoke of a Europe 'from the Atlantic to the Urals' which would include the Soviet Union. These two visions of Europe were really not compatible, for the relationship with the EEC was close and developing (France became a full member on 1 January 1958), while that with Eastern Europe was overshadowed at all times by Soviet domination. Whatever de Gaulle may have thought, the nation states of the Soviet bloc were in no sense independent, and always followed the Moscow line. If they did not, as when Czechoslovakia tried to introduce a more 'liberal' form of communism in 1968, they were crushed by Soviet military might. Thus the invasion of Czechoslovakia by Soviet and Warsaw Pact forces in August 1968 was a painful lesson for de Gaulle. He had tried to ignore Cold War tensions between East and

West, but Czechoslovakia was a forcible reminder that they still existed. Despite western protests, the Soviet government showed no disposition to allow more freedom in its Communist satellite states.

Even inside Western Europe de Gaulle's policy was circumscribed by French national interest and his own prejudices. He was always aware of his difficult experiences with the Anglo-Americans in the Second World War, and this prejudice against 'Anglo-Saxons' was behind his decision to veto Britain's first effort to enter the EEC in January 1963. De Gaulle also claimed that his five EEC partners lacked the courage to air their objections to British entry, but there is little doubt that it was favoured by Italy and the Benelux states. He further claimed that Britain was an unsuitable candidate for membership of the EEC because she would be an American 'Trojan Horse' in Europe (i.e. an American stooge), and because her imperial links were more important to her than any links with Europe. Subsequently, in 1967, de Gaulle was to veto a second British application for membership.

Were any other factors involved in de Gaulle's decision to exclude the British from EEC membership? One was certainly a desire to keep the British out because of de Gaulle's new rapprochment with West Germany. The Franco-German Treaty of Friendship was signed in 1963 and symbolically sealed when de Gaulle and the Federal German Chancellor, Konrad Adenaeur, attended mass together at Rheims cathedral. De Gaulle wanted the EEC to be dominated by the Franco-German axis and he was certainly successful in this, but his anti-Americanism did not find an echo in West Germany which remained a strong supporter of the NATO alliance. Indeed there was fear in West Germany that too close an association with de Gaulle would endanger the all-important American alliance.

The West German treaty was popular in France. However, polls showed that French people actually favoured British EEC membership, meaning that, as so often, de Gaulle's interpretation of the national interest was peculiarly his own. As far as the EEC was concerned, this meant avoidance of true union in West Europe in favour of a loose union of 'nation states' which would remain sovereign but should (in de Gaulle's view) accept French leadership. The extract quoted above shows all de Gaulle's awareness of Europe's old traditions but he was no federalist. He never shared his old subordinate Jean Monnet's dream of a 'United States of Europe'.

c) World Affairs

From about 1966 onwards de Gaulle indulged in his role as an international statesman. There were tours of Latin America and Africa, and notoriously of Canada in 1967 when he caused an international incident by crying (in a context of French-speaking Canadians wanting far more autonomy from the English-dominated government) *'Vive le*

Quebec libre' (Long live free Quebec). A furious Canadian government ensured that de Gaulle went home early!

There were also abrupt changes of direction in policy in the later years. From a pro-Israeli position in the Middle East up to the Six Day War of 1967, France veered sharply round to a pro-Arab stance and condemned Israeli occupation of the lands she seized in the war. This may have been an attempt to secure Arab goodwill, but the new policy was never popular at home. Then in 1968-9 there was a sharp turnaround in policy towards the USA (de Gaulle had been consistently critical of American policy in Vietnam) with a successful visit to Paris in 1969 by President Nixon. Historians have suggested that the ageing general, shaken by the events of 1968 at home, may have seen increased merit in strengthening ties with Washington. It was a typical Gaullist paradox that the General could be very critical of aspects of American policy, yet be the first at America's side when crisis threatened (as when Soviet missiles were found in Cuba in 1962).

Yet, quirky though it often was, de Gaulle did establish a distinctive French position on world issues. More pertinently, as Julian Jackson has pointed out, de Gaulle was often remarkably prescient. He foresaw the breakup of the Soviet Empire in Eastern Europe and his criticisms of Israeli policy in the Middle East proved only too accurate. Occupation of Arab territories did indeed lead to repression and bloodshed. As the supreme nationalist, de Gaulle would certainly not have been surprised by the triumph of modern-day nationalism.

d) Decolonisation

De Gaulle has already been given credit for the granting of Algerian independence, but his contribution did not end there, for he continued the process of decolonisation begun under the Fourth Republic (see page 117). Under the Fifth Republic ten former colonies in West and Equatorial Africa and Madagascar chose to be self-governing member states of the French Union (a rough equivalent of the British Commonwealth), while five smaller colonies remained as overseas territories under direct French rule. De Gaulle also offered a third option to the former French colonies. This was complete independence, an option in fact only chosen by Guinea. Almost certainly only de Gaulle could have offered the French Empire in Africa such a choice without provoking a violent response from the French Right. It is important, however, to recognise that de Gaulle was building on the law of 1956, which had given the overseas territories local assemblies elected by universal suffrage.

An additional point is that the 1963 Yaoundé Convention granted France's former African colonies associate membership of the EEC. This both helped to secure their economic future, and maintained the link with the mother country enshrined in the concept of the French Union.

7 De Gaulle's Fall

De Gaulle was not deceived by the massive Gaullist landslide in 1968. He felt that it was more of an endorsement of Georges Pompidou than of himself (which was one of the reasons that he sacked Pompidou). He also was at odds with the more right-wing nature of the Chamber, recognising the need for educational reforms. These were implemented by the Education Minister Edgar Faure (the universities were made less bureaucratic and better funded), but there were rumblings of discontent within the Gaullist Party.

In February 1969 de Gaulle put up two reforms for approval by the French people. One was a measure for regional decentralisation of power, and the other a reform of the Senate whereby it became a purely advisory body. Neither issue was of central importance, and de Gaulle's decision to put them to a referendum seems to have been part of the process of reassuring himself that he still had majority popular support on his side. In the event, he did not, for when the referendum was held in April 1969 de Gaulle lost by a margin of 53 to 47 per cent, whereupon he resigned his position, although the constitution did not demand that he do so.

Why did de Gaulle resign in this abrupt way on such relatively minor issues? Was it his earlier feeling that all the 'heroic' deeds had been done and that the referendum defeat offered a graceful way out? He would not be seen clinging, as he grew older, to power without the real consent of the French people (in fact he still had three of his seven years of presidential term to run). Historians have been divided over the issue. Jackson has tended to the view that de Gaulle was consciously looking for a 'way out' after the trauma of 1968. His biographer, Jean de Lacouture, has made the point that de Gaulle always had before him the image of the allegedly senile Pétain who remained in power too long in a state of physical and mental decline. He inclines to the view that rather than looking for an easy exit, de Gaulle hoped to go out in a blaze of triumph. What better perhaps than a conclusive electoral victory? In the event, he did not get it, and seemed aware in the last days of the referendum campaign that he would lose.

8 Conclusion

Charles de Gaulle gave the Fifth Republic both a stability which its predecessor had not had and a distinctive voice in world affairs. But a price was paid for this in terms of authoritarianism and insensitivity to domestic grievance which erupted in the 'events' of May 1968. A leader more attuned to the warning signs would have picked them up earlier, even though de Gaulle claimed to have such a special relationship with the French people. The question must be whether de Gaulle needed to demand such a high price to achieve stability, for even when the urgent Algerian problem had been solved de Gaulle continued to treat the democratic process in a dismissive way, and to overuse the referendum with its fascist overtones (it was a favourite device of Hitler's). Yet de Gaulle's mystique remains and his legacy survives. As he himself wrote after his retirement from politics, 'The French no longer want de Gaulle. But the myth, you will see the growth of the myth in thirty years'.

To the end the paradox between the autocrat and the democrat remained. In 1946 he had quit politics in disgust because he could not stand the inter-party bickering involved in the parliamentary process. His preference always was for the vague idealism of the 'Rally of the French People' rather than for the dull reality of party politics.

Yet de Gaulle never used his immense prestige to set up a personal dictatorship which might have been possible in the turbulent environment of the late 1950s. This persistent ambivalence was reflected in the circumstances of his final resignation. On the one hand he planned to devolve responsibility for many local matters to new regional councils, but on the other he wanted to reduce the powers of the Senate. Many French people felt that this would mean a movement in the direction of dictatorship, because the Senate already represented local interests. The proposals, therefore, almost cancelled each other out, and it was clear that the General was really asking for a vote of confidence in himself.

This he did not get, but the defeat did not mean that the French people had forgotten their debt to him. In the war he had kept the flame of resistance alive and preserved France's honour. After it he had united a divided country and presided over the birth of the Fourth Republic even if he subsequently disagreed with the direction it took. He had then ended the disastrous Algerian war and given France eleven years of domestic stability. Arguably he was the single most significant figure produced by his country in the twentieth century.

Making notes on 'The Fifth Republic, 1958-69'

The chapter follows a chronological approach in its analysis of the principal features of the first 11 years of the Fifth Republic, although there are separate sections on domestic and foreign policies. You are advised to follow the same sort of pattern when making notes, which will need to be quite detailed if you are studying this topic for examination purposes.

The following headings and questions will help you arrange your ideas in a way which will be easy to follow when you need to consult your notes.

1   De Gaulle's Background
1.1 His family background.
1.2 His patriotism and military experience.

Gaullism
What it meant
Impact on foreign policy
Impact on domestic policy

Politics
Constitutional. Parliament and Presidency -
De Gaulle's personal role
The authoritarianism leading to 1968 events
Constitutional reforms rejected

Economics
Indicative planning and four-year policy
Rapid growth rate and industrialisation
Unpopular with public

The Algerian War
De Gaulle's evolutionary policy
Resistance from Army and *colons* - attitude of FLN
The Algerian settlement and peace

Foreign Policy
De Gaulle's concept of France's role
The independent French deterrent
Withdrawal from NATO
French attitude to EEC - de Gaulle bars British entry
Importance of Franco-German alliance
Decolonisation
Personal nature of de Gaulle's foreign policy

Summary - The Fifth Republic, 1958-69

Answering essay questions on 'The Fifth Republic, 1958-69'

This period appears to be dominated by the personality of Charles de Gaulle, but study of the seven main sections of this chapter, as listed in the note-making section, makes it clear that there are other central issues. It is possible to pose a number of questions:

    1a What do you understand by the term Gaullism? Discuss the view that it offered no distinctive solution to France's domestic problems.

1b 'A certain idea of France.' How did de Gaulle's idea of France influence his conduct of policy between 1958 and 1969?

2a De Gaulle said he would not 'content himself with opening chrysanthemum shows'. How then did his presidential role differ from that of his predecessors in the Fourth Republic?

2b In what ways did the roles of Parliament and the presidency appear to clash under the Fifth Republic?

3a 'Algeria blocks everything.' In what sense was de Gaulle's handling of the Algerian Question influenced by this judgement?

3b Assess the role played by the French Army in the Algerian Question between 1958 and 1962.

4a Why was the economic policy of the Fifth Republic so apparently successful but lacking in popular support?

4b 'Neither as great as the student revolutionaries made out nor yet as slight as the Communists claimed.' Discuss this view of the events of 1968.

5a Was de Gaulle's foreign policy motivated by jealousy or patriotism?

5b 'A Europe from the Atlantic to the Urals.' Was de Gaulle's concept of Europe anything more than a utopian dream?

6a 'A stultifyingly centralized and authoritarian system.' Is this a fair verdict on de Gaulle's Fifth Republic?

6b 'The politics of grandeur were always designed more for domestic than for foreign ends.' Discuss this view of de Gaulle's policies.

The pivotal question here is 6b) which demands an assessment of both de Gaulle's domestic and foreign policies. Do not be put off by the challenging nature of the quotation, as students often are. In reality the examiner is getting you to think about the important link between domestic and foreign policy, which is always there but perhaps more acutely so under de Gaulle. Another way of phrasing this question might be 'Was de Gaulle's ambitious foreign policy as much for domestic consumption as for impressing foreigners?' It demands both a knowledge of the motivation behind de Gaulle's policies (linking up here with 1a) and 1b)) and the foreign and domestic pressures he was under.

A useful way of approaching this essay, at the vital planning stage, would be to draw up two lists of aims and objectives for de Gaulle's domestic and foreign policies. You could then note the degree to which the two overlap. Consideration would also need to be given to what you understand by the term 'politics of grandeur'. These are the key words in the question. If you don't understand them then you will flounder, but this is true of any essay question.

Source-based questions on 'The Fifth Republic, 1958-69'

1 Gaullism

Study the extract from de Gaulle's memoirs on page 122. Answer the following questions.

a) According to de Gaulle what was special about France's position in the world? (5 marks)

b) Using your own knowledge and the evidence in the passage, show how de Gaulle refused to allow events to disturb his vision of France. (5 marks)

c) From your reading of the source, assess whether foreign or domestic policy was likely to be the dominant component in Gaullism. Explain your answer. (5 marks)

2 Europe

Read the extract from de Gaulle's memoirs on page 135. Answer the following questions.

a) Using your own knowledge and the evidence in the source, outline the difference between de Gaulle's two concepts of Europe. (4 marks)

b) Explain what you understand by the term 'a concert of European states'. (2 marks)

c) From your knowledge, evaluate whether de Gaulle's European policy did indeed increase the 'interdependence and solidarity' of the European states. (9 marks)

CHAPTER 8

Conclusion

1 The Continuity in French History, 1914-69

As the introduction to this book suggested, the history of France under 'the Three Republics' was one of turbulence and change. This makes it easy to overlook the important ways in which there was a good deal of continuity and stability in France.

Stability is obvious in some areas. Until the end of the Second World War, for example, France was still a largely agrarian society. Indeed the 1936 census showed that 37 per cent of the working population was still engaged in farming or allied occupations (by comparison Britain had this figure back in 1800).

The French population, at around 40 millions barely changed between 1870 and 1940 (the military implications of this were pointed out in the introduction). Earlier chapters have also provided evidence about the conservativism of the French education system which made social mobility difficult. In social terms, therefore, for much of the period under examination France was a profoundly conservative society.

Reference has been made in the introduction and in Chapter 3 to the Andrew thesis on political stability in France during the period between 1914 and 1969, and this provides significant evidence to counteract the old stereotype of France as an unstable, almost ungovernable country.

Other historians might argue that Andrew ignores other factors like education and ideology. It is certainly true, for example, that until 1936 the French Socialist Party was reluctant to take office for ideological reasons. It did not want to be in a coalition with so-called 'bourgeois' parties. It continued to believe that France's wealthy élite would subvert any genuinely left-wing government. Nevertheless, Andrew does present an impressive case for a marked degree of political continuity under the Third Republic, and the same continuity of personnel can also be observed under the Fourth Republic. Indeed Andrew goes on to argue that it was France's social stability and provincialism which caused the constant changes of government. Because voters and politicians (many of whom doubled as mayors and deputies in Parliament – something unknown in Britain) were more interested in local politics than national politics, it was hard before 1958 to form disciplined national parties in the English style. A supporting argument is that French people, because of their revolutionary tradition and suspicion of government power, tended to vote in the first instance for deputies who would keep an eye on a probably corrupt government. In effect, the French were trying to elect an opposition rather than a government. It is certainly true that twentieth-century French history is littered with scandals, which might indeed have made the electorate suspicious and anti-government. The existence of movements like

Poujadism in the 1950s perhaps support this view of French electoral behaviour. It is certainly not the case, as Christopher Andrew points out, that the French electoral system was to blame for the rapid turnover of governments. Virtually the same one has operated since 1958 and has produced much more governmental stability.

Where else can we find continuity under the 'Three Republics'? A disposition to support authoritarian rule was noted in the introduction, which might well have evolved from the evidence that the existing system was not able to cope. In 1940, for example, even the Socialists voted in favour of the authoritarian Marshal Pétain, and against their own democratic Third Republic. Other historians like Stanley Hoffman would see this final rejection of the Third Republic as evidence of the fragmentation of the old system.

Conversely, another characteristic of the Third Republic between 1914 and 1940 was the way it invariably excluded the Left from power. Even when the Left did come to power in 1936-7, it was convinced that the 'two hundred families' would bring about its downfall. The dominance of conservatism is a consistent feature of this period and its post-war sequel. Only in 1981 was an authentic left-wing government to achieve power in France again. This adds weight to the argument that French society remained innately conservative in the post-war decades as well, and leaves open the question of whether France, as Léon Blum charged, was and is ruled by the bourgeoisie.

2 Turning Points

If there was continuity, there was also change under the Three Republics: 1940 was certainly a watershed because France's military collapse brought in its wake the downfall of the Third Republic. But most historians would now agree that the rejection of the Third Republic was a recognition of the fact that its institutions had been failing for a long time. It was not, however, true that political decline brought about military defeat, rather that France's military defeat caused a recognition of her political deficiencies.

Unfortunately 1940 afforded an opportunity in the short run not for reform, but for the anti-republican forces in France to have their day on the coat tails of Nazi tyranny. In doing so, both the traditional Right and the fascist far Right, as Hoffman points out, showed themselves to be more pro-German than French. France's problems were not to be solved by becoming part of Hitler's 'New Order'. As it was, Hoffman argues, the painful lesson learnt from the Second World War was that the settling of accounts (with the Rightists at Vichy taking revenge on the Left) in French politics was ultimately counterproductive. After the bloodshed of the *'épuration'*, the post-war period was to be notable for a burying of hatchets, and ultimately even an amnesty for Vichyites.

The other great turning point was in 1958. Again there was a profound crisis, this time caused by the Algerian war. France had not been defeated, but her society was bitterly divided about the morality of the struggle against the FLN. Once more, the French turned to an authoritarian figure but this time to give them a new long-lasting constitution, and a stable governmental system. De Gaulle achieved both, and succeeded in giving France the strong executive presidency which the founding fathers of the Third Republic had actually wanted in the 1870s. In the event, matters came out back to front then - leaving the country with a President who, in the popular phrase, just wore evening dress in the daytime and had no real power. Perhaps the best tribute to de Gaulle's reforms is that they endured both under the period of right-wing domination from 1958 to 1981, and under that of the Left from 1981 to 1993.

Change in France has not just been constitutional. Her large colonial empire has been given its independence (all bar a few small dependencies). This again was largely the achievement of de Gaulle. Decolonisation went hand-in-hand with a new European role for France which became a dominant partner in the EC. This achievement, based on the Schuman Plan of 1950 and Franco-German rapprochement, itself marks a profound change from the past. In 1914, France fought Germany and was bled white. In 1940 she was defeated and occupied by her. But by 1963, Charles de Gaulle and Konrad Adenaeur were praying together in Rheims Cathedral as friends and allies. That was something that Aristide Briand might have hoped for, but could not be achieved in the 1920s because of the burden of the past and then the explosion of German fascism in the 1930s.

It is a final irony, perhaps, that imperial France was replaced by industrial France which now has no global pretensions. Better economic management after 1945, initially based on indicative planning, changed France forever. No longer was she a country of peasants and vineyards, though both still exist, but a thrusting industrial power devoted to the concept of European integration.

The French have a saying, 'Plus ça change, plus c'est la même chose' (the more things change, the more they stay the same). They are still an intensely patriotic nation, proud of their history and culture, and their republican traditions. But in every other respect, the France of today bears scant resemblance to that of 1914 or 1940.

In 1969 when General de Gaulle retired from politics, it was not clear that the institutions of the Fifth Republic would prove to be more durable than those of the Third or Fourth. But the omens were good, and the bigger questions were posed in the area of foreign policy, where de Gaulle's style had been confrontational. Would 'la grand nation' finally accept the status of a second-class power and concentrate on developing its economy? Would the Fifth Republic outlive the charismatic leadership of its founder and survive under more pragmatic, earthbound men? French politics then, as always, were never dull.

Using the 'Conclusion'

The conclusion offers three main arguments:

1) Despite the changes brought about by two world wars, there is a considerable degree of continuity in French history during this period.
2) That 1940 and 1958 were significant watersheds in modern French history.
3) During the period 1914-1969 France has made the shift away from being an imperial power with a predominantly agrarian economy to being a major industrial power closely integrated with its Western European neighbours.

In all three cases, you will need to establish the criteria you will use to make judgements on these issues. You will certainly need to refer back to the notes you have made on earlier chapters to refresh your memory on crucial facts and the conclusions you came to on individual issues. Consider the question, 'Assess the extent to which France's defeat in 1940 was a result of political and economic, rather than military factors.' This may well involve a review of all the material in the book, because the experience of 1914-18 may (arguably) have affected French behaviour in 1940.

This can be hard work. Thinking is harder work than learning facts, but you can't understand the issues without real thought. You will argue that you must know the facts too, but this must be done for a purpose. The process of learning the facts about inter-war French history contributes to the judgement about whether indeed military, political or economic factors predominated in France's 1940 defeat.

Chronological Table

1914	28 June	Assassination of Archduke Franz-Ferdinand at Sarajevo.
	16-23 July	Visit of Poincaré to Russia.
	1 Aug	German declaration of war on France.
	5-12 Sept	Battle of the Marne.
1916	21 Feb	Beginning of the Battle of Verdun.
	1 July-Sept	Battle of the Somme.
	Dec	Nivelle appointed Commander-in-Chief.
1917	March:	Fall of Briand government. Ribot ministry.
	16 April	Nivelle offensive.
	May	Mutinies in French army. Appointment of Pétain.
	Nov	Clemenceau government.
1918	Mar-July	Ludendorff offensive.
	18 July	Allied counter-offensive led by Foch.
	11 Nov	Armistice.
1919	28 June	Treaty of Versailles signed.
	Nov	Victory of National Block in Assembly elections.
1920	Jan	Clemenceau defeated in presidential election.
	Dec	Split between Communists and Socialists at Tours.
1921		Trade union split between CGT and CGTU.
1922	Jan	Government of Poincaré.
1923	Jan	Occupation of the Ruhr by French troops.
1924	May	Election victory of Cartel des Gauches.
	Oct	Dawes Plan.
1925	April	Resignation of Herriot.
	Oct	Treaty of Locarno signed.
1925-32		Briand Foreign Minister.
1926	May	Government of Poincaré - decree laws introduced.
1928		Decision to build Maginot Line made.
1929	July	Retirement of Poincaré
	Oct	Wall Street Crash.
1930	June	French evacuation of Rhineland.
1932	May	Election of Herriot government.
1933	Jan	Hitler became German Chancellor.
	July	Four Power Pact.
		Stavisky Affair.
1934	6 Feb	Attack on National Assembly in Paris.
	9 Oct	Assassination of Barthou and King Alexander.

1935	April	Stresa agreement.
	May	Franco-Soviet Treaty signed.
	Dec	Hoare-Laval Agreement.
1936	Mar	Remilitarisation of Rhineland by Hitler.
	April-May	Chamber elections, victory of Popular Front.
		Matignon agreements.
	Oct	Devaluation of franc.
		Beginning of Spanish Civil War.
1937	March	Léon Blum announced 'pause'.
	June	Fall of Blum government.
1938	April	Daladier government formed.
	Sept	Munich Agreement.
	Oct	Paul Reynaud became Finance Minister.
1939	Mar	Dismemberment of Czechoslovakia by Hitler.
	12 Aug	Anglo-French mission to Moscow.
	23 Aug	Nazi-Soviet Pact.
	1 Sept	German invasion of Poland.
	3 Sept	Britain and France declared war on Germany.
1940	20 Mar	Reynaud succeeded Daladier as Prime Minister.
	10 May	German invasion of France and Low Countries.
	13-14 May	French front broken on River Meuse.
	19 May	Pétain entered government.
	29 May-4 June	Dunkirk evacuation.
	14 June	Paris fell.
	22 June	Armistice with Germany.
	3 July	British attack on French fleet at Mers-el-Kébir.
	Oct	Hitler-Pétain interview at Montoire.
1941	Feb	Darlan in charge of government.
1942	April	Riom trials. Laval returned to power.
	11 Nov	Germans moved into unoccupied zone.
		French fleet scuttled at Toulon.
	June	Committee of National Liberation formed.
1944	6 June	Allied landing in Normandy.
	26 Aug	De Gaulle entered Paris.
1945	21 Oct	Referendum ending Third Republic.
1946	January	De Gaulle resigned as head of state.
	May	Electorate voted against First Constitution.
	June	Election of Second Constituent Assembly.
	Oct	Second Constitution accepted by referendum.
1947	Mar	Anglo-French Dunkirk Treaty.
	May	Prime Minister Ramadier sacked Communist ministers.
1948	Jan	Formation of so-called 'Third Force'.

1949	April	NATO Treaty signed.
1950	May	Robert Schuman's coal and steel plan.
1951	April	Coal and steel agreement between France, Germany, Italy and Benelux.
1953		Poujadist League formed.
1954	May	Fall of Dien Bien Phu.
	June	Government of Mendés-France formed.
	July	Indo-China settlement approved by French Assembly but EDC Treaty rejected.
	Nov	Algerian revolt.
1956	Mar	Independence of Morocco and Tunisia recognised.
	Nov	Suez intervention.
1957	Mar	Treaty of Rome, bringing France into the EEC.
1958	13 May	Revolt of Europeans and army in Algeria.
	1 June	Government of General de Gaulle accepted by Assembly.
	21 Dec	De Gaulle elected President.
1959	8 Jan	De Gaulle proclaimed President of the Fifth Republic.
1960	Feb	First French nuclear bomb exploded.
1961	Jan	Referendum on future of Algeria.
	April	Army revolt in Algeria collapsed.
1962	July	Algerian independence proclaimed.
	Dec	Cuban Missile crisis.
1963	14 Jan	De Gaulle vetoed first British application to join the EEC.
	23 Jan	Franco-German Treaty signed.
1965	Dec	De Gaulle elected for second presidential term.
1966	Mar	France withdraws from NATO.
1967	Nov	De Gaulle's second veto on Britain's EEC application.
1968	10-11 May	Massive student demonstrations against regime.
	19 May	De Gaulle's 'flight' to Germany.
	30 May	Dissolution of National Assembly.
	23-30 June	Gaullist election victories.
1969	27 April	Resignation of de Gaulle after defeat in referendum.
1970	9 Nov	Death of Charles de Gaulle.

Further Reading

It would be helpful if you spent some time reading relevant chapters on the general history of France during this period. The most accessible existing texts, although none are easy reads, are: C. Andrew, 'Chaos and Stability: Third French Republic 1870-1940', Vol. 2, No. 3, *(Modern History Review,* February 1991).

A. Cobban, *A History of Modern France,* Volume III, (Pelican 1965), is useful, although now rather dated and too diffuse for most.

F. Giles, *The Locust Years. The Story of the Fourth French Republic,* (Secker and Warburg 1991), provides a readable history of the Fourth Republic, although it will be too detailed for all but the real enthusiast.

P. Goubert, *The Course of French History,* (Routledge 1988).

J.F. MacMillan, *Politics and Society in Twentieth-Century France,* (Edward Arnold 1992).

R. Price, *A Concise History of France,* (Cambridge University Press 1993).

Biographies

J. Jackson, *Charles de Gaulle,* (Coronet 1990) is well-written, concise and accessible.

J. Laucouture, *De Gaulle,* (Seuil, 3 vols, 1984-6) is very sympathetic to its subject but too detailed for the great majority of students.

Specialist Studies

Most of these will be too detailed for all but in depth studies, but there is one book on foreign policy which could be helpful if used with care:

A. Adamthwaite, *France and the Coming of the Second World War,* (Frank Cass 1977).

Index